And on the Seventh Day:
Faculty Consulting and Supplemental Income

by Carol M. Boyer and Darrell R. Lewis

ASHE-ERIC Higher Education Report No. 3, 1985

Prepared by

® *Clearinghouse on Higher Education*
The George Washington University

Published by

ASHE

Association for the Study of Higher Education

Jonathan D. Fife,
Series Editor

1987

Cite as
Boyer, Carol M. and Lewis, Darrell R. *And on the Seventh Day:
Faculty Consulting and Supplemental Income*. ASHE-ERIC
Higher Education Report No. 3. Washington, D.C.: Association
for the Study of Higher Education, 1985.

The ERIC Clearinghouse on Higher Education invites individuals
to submit proposals for writing monographs for the Higher Education Report series. Proposals must include:
1. A detailed manuscript proposal of not more than five pages.
2. A 75-word summary to be used by several review committees
   for the initial screening and rating of each proposal.
3. A vita.
4. A writing sample.

Library of Congress Catolog Card Number 85-072834
ISSN 0884-0040
ISBN 0-913317-22-5

ERIC® **Clearinghouse on Higher Education**
The George Washington University
One Dupont Circle, Suite 630
Washington, D.C. 20036

ASHE **Association for the Study of Higher Education**
One Dupont Circle, Suite 630
Washington, D.C. 20036

This publication was partially prepared with funding from the
National Institute of Education, U.S. Department of Education
under contract no. 400-82-0011. The opinions expressed in this
report do not necessarily reflect the positions or policies of NIE
or the Department.

EXECUTIVE SUMMARY

Faculty consulting has long been recognized as legitimate expression of the traditional faculty role and mission of most academic institutions. Recently, however, concern about the appropriateness of faculty consulting and other activities producing supplemental income has increased as such activity reportedly has increased, as public sentiment toward postsecondary education has changed, and as greater accountability has been called for. The central concern appears to be whether faculty consulting and other supplemental income activities result in "shirking . . . [other] university responsibilities" (Patton 1980). The basis for such concern is not with the earning of supplemental income per se, but with the earning of supplemental income on university time—what some observers perceive as "double dipping."

On the one side are those who argue that faculty consulting might result in neglect of students and other university responsibilities, abuses of academic freedom, conflicts of interest, and illegitimate use of institutional resources. On the other side are those who argue that faculty consulting enhances both research and teaching, that conflicts of interest and other abuses are very uncommon, and that faculty consulting benefits both the institution and society as well as the individual.

Until recently, much of the argument both for and against outside professional consulting has been inconclusive because of the anecdotal or speculative nature of evidence that could be brought to bear on the nature, the intent, or the extent of such activity. To complicate matters further, faculty consulting often has been grouped with "other moonlighting activities." To address public and institutional concern about faculty consulting and to inform policy deliberations on such activity, it is important to discriminate between consulting and all other activities that generate supplemental income.

In view of current economic and demographic conditions as well as forecasts for higher education, the debate and policy concerns about faculty consulting and other supplemental income activities are likely to intensify. Basically, the debate involves six important issues:

1. Who are the faculty who consult?
2. Is faculty consulting increasing?

3. Are faculty who consult shirking their responsibilities on campus?
4. Are faculty exploiting their consulting opportunities to substantially increase their total earnings?
5. Are faculty motivated to consult primarily for economic reasons?
6. Are most institutional policies and procedures adequate for governing faculty consulting and other activities producing supplemental income?

In addressing these issues, this report has three additional, related objectives: first, to extend existing knowledge about outside professional consulting as a faculty activity—where it is done, how much of it, by whom, and with what benefits and costs; second, to contribute further to our understanding of the role of supplemental income vis-à-vis the division of academic labor both among and within institutions; and third, to contribute to more informed policy development and decision making concerning these matters within colleges and universities.

No useful theory presently exists that relates outside professional consulting to the traditional mission of most academic institutions in the United States. Yet consulting consistently emerges as part of the academic role. Most of the research on the academic profession has been guided by the traditional mission and functions of colleges and universities: research, teaching, and service. These three functions overlap considerably of course (with the service function frequently considered a distant third behind teaching and research in most institutions). It is in the context of this service function that consulting appears. Faculty consulting can be defined as the application of one's professional and scholarly expertise in the community outside the academic institution. Viewed as the natural extension of one's teaching and research activities, both the service function and consulting activities long have been recognized as legitimate expressions of the traditional faculty role and mission of most academic institutions in the United States. Moreover, just as graduate instruction has multiple benefits, so too does faculty consulting have multiple benefits whenever it also extends and reinforces the teaching and research expertise of individual faculty members.

Who Are the Faculty Who Consult?
The evidence presented in this report shows that, compared to their faculty colleagues who do not consult, faculty who consult for pay are more likely to be employed in universities than in colleges, to hold higher academic rank, to have higher base salaries, to be among the more distinguished faculty, and to be from one of the professional fields or the sciences.

Is Faculty Consulting Increasing?
Data from a number of institutional and national surveys indicate that, contrary to conventional wisdom, faculty consulting does not appear to be increasing appreciably, even though *real* faculty salaries have significantly declined in the past decade or so. From the research literature, it appears that approximately 35 to 50 percent of all faculty devote some portion of their time to professional consulting over the course of any two-year period, with only 15 to 20 percent consulting during a given academic year. Further, it appears that these proportions have remained relatively constant during the past decade.

Are Faculty Who Consult Shirking Their Responsibilities on Campus?
The available evidence clearly suggests that those faculty who do consult are, on average, at least as active in their other faculty roles as their peers who do not consult. Faculty who consult, compared to their peers who do not, teach as many courses and devote as much of their professional work time to teaching and research, pay more attention to issues of national importance, publish more, subscribe to more professional journals, are more satisfied with their careers and their institutions, and are at least as active in departmental and institutional governance. Further, only about 5 to 6 percent of all faculty report consulting more than one day per week. In short, it seems that faculty who do consult do so *not* at the expense of their other institutional responsibilities.

Are Faculty Exploiting Their Consulting Opportunities to Substantially Increase Their Total Earnings?

Sixty to 85 percent of all faculty report receiving some income beyond their base academic salaries. Supplemental income results from all forms of income-generating activities (for example, research and teaching during the summer months as well as consulting) and is earned both within and without the institution. The amount represents only about 15 percent of average basic academic salaries. About half of all college and university faculty report having some form of "outside" supplemental income during a given year. As for consulting specifically, it is estimated that half of all college and university faculty consult for pay at least once over the course of two years, including summers. Less than 10 percent of college and university faculty employed in fields allied with science and engineering report supplemental earnings that represent more than one-third of their base academic salaries. The comparable figure for faculty employed in the humanities is only 4 percent. Overall, however, less than half of all supplemental income has been attributed to professional consulting during the academic year. Moreover, even for those science, engineering, and humanities faculty who actually report consulting activities during the academic year, supplemental earnings represent only 20 to 25 percent of their base academic salaries. It seems, then, that most faculty are not earning large amounts of supplemental income from consulting or other outside professional activities.

Are Faculty Motivated to Consult Primarily for Economic Reasons?

Despite the significant decline in real faculty salaries over the past decade, increasing numbers of faculty are *not* being induced to seek outside professional consulting opportunities to supplement their base academic salaries, nor are they substantially increasing their supplemental incomes. Both the steady proportion of total faculty earnings accounted for by supplemental income and the steady proportion of faculty who consult are consistent with the additional finding that, among faculty who do consult, the percentage of professional work time devoted to consulting is not related to base academic salary. These findings are particularly important because they challenge much of the current conventional wisdom about faculty consulting. Recent popular and policy-related literature, for example, implies that faculty consulting is primarily motivated by economic concerns. In fact, it appears that most faculty are motivated by other important factors, such as potential benefits to their careers, potential benefits to their instruction and research, and social demand.

Are Most Institutional Policies and Procedures Adequate for Governing Faculty Consulting and Other Activities Producing Supplemental Income?

In a large number of academic institutions across the country today, such policies and procedures often fail to formally address many important considerations. Even in those institutions where the policies are fairly specific with regard to limitations, the procedures for implementing the policies and for monitoring the outside professional activities of individual faculty members often are lacking. On the other hand, in some institutions the policies and procedures are unnecessarily restrictive and even unmanageable. In sum, more explicit and carefully developed institutional policies and procedures governing faculty consulting and other activities producing supplemental income clearly are in order.

What Are the Implications for Further Research?

The literature on faculty consulting and other supplemental income activities indicates that further research is necessary in at least four important areas. First, communication and collaboration are lacking among the various national agencies collecting similar kinds of survey data on faculty, which in turn has limited the utility and comparability of such data. Second, although the literature does provide a fairly complete picture of the overall incidence and extent of faculty consulting for different time periods, little is known about individual patterns of faculty consulting over time and careers. Third, little is known about whether the opportunity cost of outside professional activities is to leisure (and therefore is borne by the individual) or to the institution. Finally, it is not clear how outside professional consulting influences faculty behavior and activities in the academic institution. The nature and extent to which faculty are influenced in their research priorities and academic objectivity by their outside professional relationships are almost wholly unexplored in the research literature.

ADVISORY BOARD

CONSULTING EDITORS

Robert Atwell
President
American Council on Education

Robert Cope
Professor of Higher Education
University of Washington

Robert L. Craig
Former Vice President, Government Affairs
American Society for Training and Development, Inc.

John W. Creswell
Associate Professor
Department of Educational Administration
University of Nebraska

W. Lee Hansen
Professor
Department of Economics
University of Wisconsin

David Kaser
Professor
School of Library and Information Science
Indiana University

George Keller
Senior Vice President
Barton-Gillet Company

David W. Leslie
Professor and Chair
Department of Educational Leadership
The Florida State University

Linda Koch Lorimer
Associate General Counsel
Yale University

Ernest A. Lynton
Commonwealth Professor and Senior Associate
Center for the Study of Policy and the Public Interest
University of Massachusetts

CONTENTS

FOREWORD

Faculty consulting has often been viewed as the most immediate means of knowledge transfer from academic institutions to the community at large. Clearly, private and public organizations benefit from being able to hire faculty members on a part-time, consulting basis. What is not as obvious is whether the relationship is also beneficial to the colleges and universities that employ the faculty full-time. Do academic institutions gain from having their faculty members interact with outside agencies? Are the stated goals and values of an higher education institution served by faculty consulting?

Another consideration is the cost to the institution. While pursuing outside activities, faculty consultants make use of resources put at their disposal by the universities—offices, telephones, and mailings. Is the university obligated to allow its faculty free run on its resources as long as the work is at least tangentially useful to the institution? Where should administrators draw the line between the legitimate use of faculty prerogatives and abuse? In order to examine these and related issues, it is necessary to consider the mission of colleges and universities and how expected faculty contributions help realize it.

Faculty duties traditionally relate to teaching, research, and service. Within this framework of responsibility, is faculty consulting a legitimate expression of the research and service functions? And to what degree does consulting aid or hinder the teaching function? Assuming that the benefits to the individual may be separate from any benefits to the university, to what extent should consulting work be viewed as compatible with any member's obligation to the institution? Consultants certainly gain professionally and personally from outside work, but do their institutions also benefit from their enhanced expertise? A more disturbing issue is whether professors find it *necessary* to supplement their base salaries by engaging in outside work?

In examining these questions, this report addresses the legitimacy of faculty consulting within the realm of academic responsibility. The authors, Carol Boyer, senior policy analyst at the Education Commission of the States, and Darrell Lewis, associate dean of education at the University of Minnesota, have long been interested in the economics of education. To study the dynamics of faculty consulting, they surveyed available literature and analyzed the disparate sources of information. They point out the obstacles to reaching definitive conclusions. It is always difficult to distinguish between personal and professional time for faculty members, as shown consistently in faculty workload studies. The nature of scholarly work is that there is often overlap between business and pleasure. Faculty consulting has even more areas of gray, if you will, where institutional responsibility and personal gain overlap or collide.

This report, the third in the 1985 ASHE-ERIC series, offers some surprising answers. However, it may prompt other questions: To what degree should administrators hold faculty members accountable for their consulting work? How tenuous a relationship must exist between faculty consulting and the defined faculty role within the academic community before administrators should exercise their authority? Faculty members who already consult or are considering consulting, as well as administrators active in faculty and staffing decisions, will benefit greatly from this thoughtful report.

Jonathan D. Fife
Series Editor
Professor and Director
ERIC Clearinghouse on Higher Education
The George Washington University

CONCEPTUAL FRAMEWORK AND DEFINITION

The ultimate purpose of this report is to address the policy question of whether institutional guidelines governing faculty consulting and other activities producing supplemental income ought to be more or less restrictive. First, however, the potential benefits—to the individual, to the institution, and to society—and the potential costs of such activities must be examined and understood. To do so requires a conceptual framework, an understanding of the related empirical research, and an understanding of what is taking place in practice. This introductory section provides a conceptual framework and historical context that relate consulting and other faculty activities to the traditional mission of most academic institutions. It also describes and distinguishes between outside professional consulting and other activities producing supplemental income.

Conceptual Framework

At present, no paradigm relates outside professional consulting—or, for that matter, many other faculty activities—to the traditional mission of most academic institutions in the United States. Moreover, as recently as 1978, it was argued that "there is no real tradition of studies of the professoriate with an established literature or with accepted methodological procedures" (Altbach 1978, p. 24). Thus, except for an occasional reference in a few major studies of faculty and faculty work, the literature on faculty consulting consists primarily of rhetorical exercises largely uninformed by systematic collection or analysis of data. And they are usually written by individuals who wish to object to current practice or by "institutional researchers" driven, not by theory, but by a need for concrete data to support policy development and decision making.

This lack of theory on which to base research and evaluate its results is recognized as a weakness that has kept "the sociology of the academic profession from maturing as a science" (Light 1974, pp. 2–3). In the absence of theory, most of the research on the academic profession has been guided by the conceptual division of academic functions into research, teaching, and service (see, for example (Caplow and McGee 1958; Fulton and Trow 1974; Ladd and Lipset 1975a; Wilson 1942). Because of this lack of theory and because these three functions do constitute the traditional mission of most academic institutions in the United States, this report on faculty consulting and other activities producing supplemental income uses the three functions of research, teaching, and service as its conceptual framework.

Historical Context

The closing years of the nineteenth century brought about the most sweeping transformation in the history of American higher education (see, for example, Jencks and Riesman 1968). Having completed advanced studies abroad, American scholars returned to the United States, bringing with them the German idea of a university—including notions about research, research methodology, academic freedom, and academic ranking. The growth of research that followed produced basic, albeit gradual, changes in the structure of American higher education. Yale awarded the first Ph.D. in 1861, but it was not until Johns Hopkins was founded in 1876 that the German idea of a research university was first institutionalized.

About the same time that the German university began attracting large numbers of American scholars to its doors, the accelerating forces of the Industrial Revolution gave increasing practical significance to the expertise found in colleges and universities, and Abraham Lincoln signed the Morrill Land Grant Act into law. A major landmark in the development of the modern public university, the Morrill Act of 1862 granted public lands to the states, proceeds from the sale of which were to be used to provide university training in the agricultural and mechanical arts (Cheit 1975; Wolfle 1972). Even today, major land-grant universities continue to acknowledge formally their "lasting obligation to serve society by extending [their] teaching and research beyond the campus, applying [their] knowledge to the solution of problems—problems of people, of public bodies, and of industry and agriculture—wherever [their] help is needed and can be useful" (University of Minnesota 1980, p. 5). Thus, coupled with German intellectualism, the land-grant movement brought about extraordinary change as American higher education expanded its functions to include research and service.

Faculty Consulting Defined

Thus, the American university has existed since the late nineteenth century to perform three primary functions: the advancement of knowledge (research), the transmission of knowledge (teaching), and the application of knowledge (service). Today, this "familiar triumvirate of functions" (Perkins 1973) constitutes the traditional mission of most academic institutions in the United States, a mission expressed through the various activities of the faculty. The three functions overlap considerably, however; that is, if service is the application of knowledge, then presumably that knowledge is derived through research and conveyed to students through teaching. Therefore, whereas the seemliness of any particular faculty activity can be determined by historical examination, questions of institutional policy regarding that activity necessarily must be informed by empirical research that considers the implications of such policy for teaching, research, and service. It has been suggested, for example, that the best predictions for faculty behavior are most likely to come from analysis of their primary roles, with particular attention to the growing division of academic labor (Clark 1978). Until recently, however, a common theme in research on faculty work has been that such work is "divided between teaching and scholarship [that is, research], with service activities more an afterthought" (Austin and Gamson 1983, p. 20). Indeed, only 10 years ago, the service function was defined as a taboo area that had not been studied and was seldom talked about (Blackburn 1974). The service function has since been called the short leg on a three-legged stool (Martin 1977), and consulting has been identified as the principal outside professional activity in the service role—an aspect of faculty life that "remains taboo" and about which "our ignorance . . . remains enormous" (Blackburn 1978, p. 60). Today, even in practice, the service function is still considered "a distant third behind teaching and research" (Crosson 1983, p. 5) and seldom is given much, if any, weight in decisions about tenure and promotion (Euster and Weinbach 1983; Glauser and Axley 1983; Lewis and Becker 1979).

Faculty consulting, then, as defined here, is the application of professional and scholarly expertise in the commu-

Faculty consulting . . . is the application of professional and scholarly expertise in the community outside one's own academic institution. . . .

nity outside one's own academic institution and is not necessarily limited to income-generating activities. [The question of how best to develop a consulting practice is not addressed in this report. The body of literature on the topic is growing, however (see, for example, Axford 1967; Gallessich 1982; George 1976; Nocks 1982; Pilon and Bergquist 1979; Seiler and Dunning 1983).] Moreover, as the natural extension of one's teaching and/or research activities, faculty consulting is an important form of service to individuals and organizations off campus. Viewed in this way, faculty consulting long has been recognized as legitimate expression of the traditional faculty role and mission of most academic institutions in the United States (see figure 1). Moreover, just as graduate-level instruction—especially that occurring in seminars or problem courses and in working individually with graduate students on their research projects—is considered neither pure teaching nor pure research but has the quality of a joint product about it, so too faculty consulting has a similar quality whenever it both extends and reinforces the teaching or research expertise of the individual faculty member.

Finally, one must note that faculty consulting, as defined here, necessarily includes those activities that extend the professional and scholarly expertise of faculty beyond the written terms and conditions of most regular faculty contracts. Such activities typically are neither expressed nor required as part of an individual faculty member's regular responsibilities, although faculty contracts in some departments, such as agricultural extension, often do specify (and even require) certain types of consulting activity. The definition of faculty consulting in this report thus includes not only such "inload" consulting activities but also "overload" professional and scholarly activities that faculty undertake for outside agencies or institutions during the term of their regular faculty contract as well as off-campus consulting activities that take place during periods not covered by the regular faculty contract (such as during the summer months for most nine-month regular faculty). The definition does not, however, include "moonlighting" activities—that is, those that are not directly related to the

FIGURE 1
CONSULTING AS LEGITIMATE EXPRESSION OF THE
TRADITIONAL FACULTY ROLE AND MISSION OF
MOST ACADEMIC INSTITUTIONS

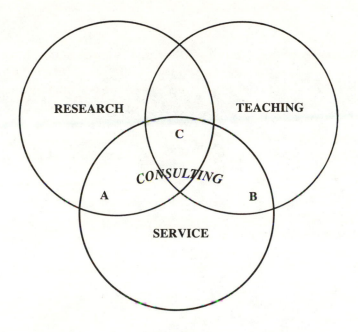

Faculty consulting, as defined here, is the extension of *research* outside the academic institution (A), the extension of *teaching* outside the academic institution (B), or the extension of *both research and teaching* outside the academic institution (C). No attempt has been made to depict the proper balance among research, teaching, and service.

Source: Boyer 1984; Dill 1982.

faculty member's profession, field of study, or discipline—as, for example, when an economist takes up farming or a forester sells insurance.

POLICY AND DECISION-MAKING FRAMEWORK

In recent years, various claims about the benefits and costs that allegedly result from faculty consulting and other supplemental income activities have appeared in the literature. Unfortunately, these claims often are made without a conceptual framework, empirical data, or both. This section addresses the issue of cost effectiveness by describing the tradeoffs involved whenever faculty effort and other institutional resources are involved in an allocation decision, by reviewing the various claims made about the benefits of faculty consulting from the perspective of who benefits (the individual, the institution, or society), and by reviewing similar claims about the costs of faculty consulting.

Tradeoffs between Costs and Benefits

Informed decisions about alternative faculty activities—as with most decisions dealing with allocations of institutional resources—should be based on estimates of cost effectiveness. Cost effectiveness usually is determined by comparing the expected costs with the expected benefits for each activity. The lower the costs for given benefits, or the greater the benefits for given costs, the greater the cost effectiveness. It is important to recognize, however, that faculty activities that are low in cost are not necessarily cost effective. Similarly, faculty activities that are cost effective are not necessarily low in cost or low in quality.

In terms of accounting, costs are defined as the total outlays likely to be spent to achieve a given set of outcomes. More generally, costs can be defined as the value of alternatives forgone to pursue a particular course of action—hence the term "opportunity costs." For example, each time an academic institution decides to approve or encourage the investment of faculty time in consulting, total outlays include both the direct costs of any institutional resource employed (for example, equipment, libraries and other facilities, supplies, faculty time) and the indirect costs of any institutional output forgone by taking faculty members away from their typical everyday activities. The presumption usually has been that consulting activities take place at the expense of forgone benefits to the institution, with faculty who do not consult providing the standard against which the regular on-campus activities of faculty who consult are compared. If, however, faculty who

consult are doing so at the expense of forgone leisure time, then the opportunity costs would be borne by the individual and not by the academic institution. Only recently has the latter issue been introduced in the literature (Boyer 1984).

Benefits, as defined here, are the opposite of costs in that they represent opportunities gained or outcomes achieved by engaging in some activity. For example, one of the principal benefits said to accrue to an academic institution when it "invests in" (that is, permits or promotes) some faculty development activity is an increase in the marginal product of its faculty that, in turn, contributes to an increase in subsequent total faculty output. Thus, it could be argued that consulting improves faculty effectiveness in subsequent teaching and research activities. (Because the marginal product of labor can be increased by a change in the quality of labor employed, consulting will yield institutional benefits if individual faculty members enhance their stock of knowledge and experience and if the institution can appropriate some or all of this increase in the marginal product of its faculty to subsequent teaching or research.) Take, for example, the economics professor who conducts a feasibility study for a new banking facility in a rural community. The study can be used as a real-world example for principles taught in her introductory economics or finance course and as the basis for a case study to illustrate important concepts or theories in her advanced courses on finance or on money and banking. The study can also be used to inform her current research efforts or to suggest new directions for further research.

Cost effectiveness, then, is a rational technique for selecting from alternative activities the activity or set of activities that will achieve either a given set of outcomes at the lowest cost or the greatest number of benefits at given costs. Determining how best to conceptualize (or define) and measure the various costs and benefits is a difficult but important task, because different conceptualizations undoubtedly will lead to different estimates of cost effectiveness. Comparisons of several such estimates can be particularly useful in situations where benefits cannot easily be specified or measured in monetary terms, as is surely the case in higher education and in most assessments of faculty consulting. [Kirschling (1979), Lewis and Kellogg (1979), Lumsden and Ritchie (1975), and Thompson (1980) have addressed these issues of specification, measurement, and analysis, especially as they relate to comparisons of cost effectiveness in higher education.]

Potential Benefits of Faculty Consulting

In recent years, various claims about the benefits of faculty consulting have appeared in the literature (see, for example, Aggarwal 1981; Allard 1982; Bok 1982; Crosson 1983; Dillon 1979b; Dillon and Bane 1980; Eddy 1981; Glauser and Axley 1983; Golomb 1979; Inman 1983; Lajoie and Weinberg 1978; Linnell 1982; Patton 1980; Redding 1983; Shulman 1980; Weston 1980–81; Wildavsky 1978). This section examines these claims from the perspective of the beneficiary—the individual, the institution, or society.

Benefits to the individual

Benefits of faculty consulting doubtless accrue to the individual faculty member who does the consulting. In addition to supplementing the faculty member's base academic salary and presumably contributing to his or her economic well-being and morale, consulting stimulates the continuing education of the faculty member. Consulting provides "an excellent route of access" to the nonacademic environment (Simon 1976) that enables the faculty member to "test academic teaching and research against real-world experience" (Aggarwal 1981, p. 17), to observe the extent to which "concepts, hypotheses, and theories hold up under the conditions of nonacademic life" (Redding 1983, p. 19), and to stay abreast of practical needs and developments in an area of expertise, a field of study, or a discipline. This exposure is especially important given the lag between discovery or innovation—whether it occurs in the private sector or the professor's laboratory or office—and publication in scholarly journals and textbooks. Typically this lag is two years for scholarly journals and from five to ten years (or more) for textbooks.

Moreover, consulting can provide the faculty member with useful information concerning sophisticated research methods and new forms of instrumentation. At the same time, by providing real-world examples for concepts and theories taught in the classroom, consulting enhances the faculty member's teaching resources. Consulting provides not only ideas and inspiration for future study or research but also external confirmation of the quality and relevance of the faculty member's expertise. And finally, consulting provides the faculty member with opportunities to interact with nonacademic colleagues in the same or related fields and to work with colleagues from other academic institutions on projects that probably could not be supported within a single academic institution.

Benefits to the institution

Most of these benefits to the individual faculty member have corresponding benefits to the employing academic institution. First, by supplementing the individual's base academic salary, consulting enables the academic institution to compete effectively in its efforts to attract and retain top professionals who have skills and expertise widely sought by business and industry. It has been claimed, for example, that it is fairly easy for faculty members in some departments (electrical engineering, for example) to as much as double their base academic salaries by consulting, on average, only one day per week. Thus, in the words of one faculty member, "eliminate faculty consulting, and either the salaries of such people become prohibitively expensive to the university, or they [the faculty members] will be lost to alternative forms of employment . . . available to them" (Golomb 1979, pp. 34–35). "In some fields talented faculty can *only* be acquired by allowing them an outside income" (Tuckman 1984, p. 432).

Under such circumstances, therefore, policies that permit consulting can be perceived as indirect salary supplement by the academic institution for purposes of "market retention"—a common practice in most American schools of medicine and business—as most academic institutions cannot compete on the basis of direct salary alone. (In fact, most major medical schools currently permit up to 100 percent of base academic salary to be supplemented by clinical and consulting practices.) When considered in this light, therefore, so long as the market rate of pay per unit of time for the outside consulting is greater than the institutional rate of pay, then such consulting will be cost effective for the institution—even if no other benefits can be identified.

Faculty consulting also complements the effectiveness of research and teaching, helps build the professional reputation of the department and university (as well as the individual faculty member), serves as an expression of service commitment to the broader community, and builds public good will toward the university (see especially Aggarwal 1981, Golomb 1979, and Patton 1980). Moreover, consulting sometimes results in work or internship experiences and postdegree career opportunities for students trained by faculty who are respected professionally outside the academic institution. Finally, consulting provides access to private-sector and government contracts as well as foundation grant monies that, in turn, aid the development of institutional resources.

Benefits to society
Some of the benefits of faculty consulting to outside agencies are fairly self-evident. Most important, faculty consulting provides both public and private agencies with access to a great pool of expertise that can be applied to a wide range of problems affecting society.

> *Just as a hospital or an auto repair shop is of value on a standby basis, even if never used, so a college or university is valuable because of the talent it has in readiness to advise on technical questions or policy issues that may arise in government at any level, in the household, on the farm, in the business firm, in the labor union, or in the school* (Bowen 1977, p. 320).

In a clearly cost-effective manner, then, agencies in society can draw on the expertise of faculty members as needed without the full costs attendant with long-term, full-time commitments. The ability of such agencies to bring in a highly qualified faculty member to address a specific problem or issue doubtless is more cost effective than attempting to attract and retain a similarly qualified individual as a full-time employee. In other words, such arrangements benefit society by "allowing academe to share *scarce* resources with the private sector" (Tuckman 1984, p. 432).

In short, "this is *talent [that] is more economical to rent than to buy*" (Golomb 1979, p. 36).

Consulting also facilitates the transfer of ideas, of research findings, and of critical judgments to the broader community and thus encourages the process of technological development (Bok 1982). "Faculty consulting is probably the most efficient mechanism imaginable through which the latest research can be incorporated into the technology" and public policy (Golomb 1979, p. 35). And finally, at least in some fields, consulting enables public and private agencies to assess the professional competence of individual faculty members and the suitability of the academic institution's educational program for their specific training needs.

Potential Costs of Faculty Consulting
Just as the various claims about benefits of faculty consulting have been recounted several times in recent years, so too the claims about the costs of faculty consulting have received considerable attention (see, for example, Aggarwal 1981; Bok 1982; Dillon 1979b; Eddy 1981; Goldberg 1983; Golomb 1979; Inman 1983; Langway and others 1978; Linnell 1982; Marver and Patton 1976; Patton 1980; Patton and Marver 1979; Weston 1980–81; Wildavsky 1978).

Foremost among the potential costs is possible neglect of students and other university responsibilities. The basis for such concern about faculty consulting is rather straightforward:

> *Today's observers are upset about what they perceive as "double-dipping" by well-paid faculty members. Their concern is not with the earnings of extra income per se; rather, these critics level their arguments at faculty members who earn outside income on university time* (Patton and Marver 1979, p. 176).

Self-determination in the use of time has long been a well-accepted part of the definition of faculty role. Nonetheless, "to many observers it appears that the availability of income-producing commitments . . . may result in faculty who choose to spend time on what pays and not necessarily on that which is of highest priority" (Dillon 1979b, p. 39).

Other potential costs of faculty consulting are possible abuses of academic freedom and conflicts of interest that result in "unconscious compromise of academic objectivity and impartiality" (Dillon 1979b, p. 39). Here the basis for concern appears to be that faculty members serving as consultants may skew the direction or outcomes of their research in ways most likely to be favorable to the agency or corporation that employs them. Such concern certainly is visible today at a number of major research centers in higher education. Recent debate has been especially strong at Stanford, Harvard, Yale, and the University of California, where many faculty members are involved in the competitive and profitable fields of bioengineering and computer electronics (Coughlin 1981; *New York Times* 1983).

Another potential cost of faculty consulting is the possible illegitimate use of institutional resources, the evidence often being the case of an individual faculty member who uses without permission university facilities, supplies, computers, or staff to support consulting activities. Still another potential cost, that of property rights, arises when consulting results in the creation of intellectual property for which the patent or copyright may rightfully belong to the university (Linnell 1982; Voegel 1977; Woodrow 1978). (Although the question of faculty ethics in relation to these matters of conflict of interest and academic freedom is not addressed in this report, a growing body of literature discusses the topic. See, for example, Clark 1978; Clark and Dillon 1982; Dillon 1979a; Freedman 1979; Hardin 1979; Linnell 1982; Schurr 1979; Schwartz 1980; Shulman 1980.)

. . . Consulting enables public and private agencies to assess the professional competence of individual faculty members. . . .

EMPIRICAL RESEARCH ON FACULTY CONSULTING

Before 1960, much of the literature on the academic profession was based on anecdotal information. Although the past two decades have witnessed a number of relatively large-scale empirical surveys of college and university faculty, research on the nature and extent of faculty work is characterized as "fragmented and rather unorganized" (Austin and Gamson 1983, p. 16). Moreover, most major surveys of faculty and faculty work have touched only tangentially on the topic of faculty consulting. Nonetheless, the data from these surveys have provided some basis for empirical research on faculty consulting. This section briefly describes four large-scale data bases and, where appropriate, also identifies subsequent studies of faculty consulting that used each data base. It also examines the reported incidence and overall extent of faculty consulting and discusses the correlates of faculty consulting, including salient characteristics of those faculty who do consult.

Large-scale Data Bases on Faculty Consulting

The first really large-scale empirical survey that included data on faculty consulting was sponsored jointly by the American Council on Education and the Carnegie Commission in 1969 (see Trow 1972 for details). This national survey included the responses of 60,028 faculty members from 303 colleges and universities that were broadly representative of American higher education. A similar, but somewhat smaller, national survey was sponsored by the Carnegie Council in 1975 (see Roizen, Fulton, and Trow 1978). This survey included the responses of 24,999 faculty members from a systematic, stratified sample of colleges and universities that was broadly representative of American higher education. These Carnegie data have since been used in one major study of faculty research activity (Fulton and Trow 1974), in a set of empirical studies of faculty consulting (Marver and Patton 1976; Patton 1980; Patton and Marver 1979), and in a study based on a subsample of these data (Lanning 1977).

Another major empirical survey that included data on faculty consulting was the *1975 Survey of the American Professoriate* (Ladd and Lipset 1975b). This national survey included the weighted responses of 3,536 full-time teaching faculty from 111 randomly selected colleges and universities. Until recently, it was the only large-scale empirical study besides the Carnegie surveys to deal with questions of faculty consulting and to include data on supplementary income. Data from that survey have since been examined in two empirical studies of faculty consulting (Dillon 1979b; Marsh and Dillon 1980) and reported in a third study (Linnell 1982).

A third, more recent survey that included data on faculty consulting was conducted by the National Science Foundation (NSF) in 1979 (Lacy and others 1981). This national survey included the weighted responses of 2,464 science and engineering faculty members from universities and four-year colleges across the country. Although a major objective of this survey was "to assess the magnitude of academic research activities more comprehensively than had been done before" (Lacy and others 1981, p. 6), some attention also was given to other faculty activities, including consulting. Although these NSF data have not been the primary source of data in any subsequent empirical studies of faculty consulting, they are discussed in one study (Boyer 1984).

The fourth and most recent large-scale survey that included data on faculty consulting was conducted by the National Research Council (NRC) in 1981 (NRC 1982). The original survey included the weighted responses of 63,022 doctorate recipients from a stratified random sample of all science, engineering, and humanities doctorates in the United States who had earned their degrees since 1938. NRC data on those respondents who were employed full time as faculty in universities or four-year colleges have since been examined in two studies of faculty consulting, with sample sizes of 9,325 (Boyer 1984) and 15,574 (Boyer and Lewis 1984).

The Extent of Faculty Consulting
This section summarizes the results of the empirical studies identified previously regarding the reported incidence and the overall extent of faculty consulting. It examines differences among studies, apparent discrepancies in results, the characteristics of faculty who consult, and the question of whether faculty who consult are shirking their other responsibilities.

What is the incidence of faculty consulting?

A summary of the 1969 Carnegie survey data indicates that 37 percent of the faculty in all fields reported having served as a paid consultant some time during the preceding two years. The range was from 17 percent for faculty in English and philosophy to 70 percent for faculty in medicine and 78 percent for faculty in clinical psychology (Ladd and Lipset 1975a, p. 351).

Based on a subsample of the 1969 Carnegie survey data base, another study (Lanning 1977) indicated that of some 8,000 faculty members at major universities who reported having "served as a paid consultant," 54 percent reported devoting some portion of their work time in a normal week to consulting during the two years before the survey (with or without pay). Sixteen percent reported devoting on average more than 10 percent of a normal week to consulting.

Yet another set of studies was based on the 1969 and 1975 Carnegie survey data. A summary of the findings from two analyses of these data (Marver and Patton 1976; Patton and Marver 1979) indicates that the proportion of college and university faculty who reported consulting for pay over a 24-month period did not change between 1969 and 1975: 37 percent of the faculty consulted for pay during an average week, 19 percent consulted on average more than one half-day per week, and only 6 percent consulted on average more than one day per week (Patton 1980).

Analysis of the 1975 Ladd and Lipset survey data, on the other hand, shows that nearly half of all college and university faculty reported some paid consulting activity for the preceding two-year period (Linnell 1982; Marsh and Dillon 1980). Subsequent Ladd and Lipset surveys showed that "faculty elites" (that is, elected members of distinguished national academies) who were under 70 years of age were far more likely than their faculty colleagues in major research universities to report having served as consultants to federal government agencies and national corporations (Lipset 1982). The latter finding is consistent with the Carnegie survey finding that the most active researchers (that is, five or more publications in the two years preceding the survey) were more likely than their less active faculty colleagues to report having done some consulting—paid or unpaid—in that same two-year period (Fulton and Trow 1974).

The studies reported thus far were based almost entirely on the Carnegie or the Ladd-Lipset data bases. Nonetheless, some of the results appear to be inconsistent. Such inconsistency could be the result of differences among studies in sampling techniques, questionnaires, or research methods. It is important to note, too, that none of the studies are recent enough to reflect any change in paid consulting activity that could be attributed to recent demographic or economic changes in higher education.

More recent data on the faculty consulting of science and engineering faculty in universities and four-year colleges can be found in the 1981 NSF survey (Lacy and others 1981). The NSF survey data indicate that all science and engineering faculty as a group reported devoting less than 2.5 percent of their professional work time to paid or unpaid consulting activities (that is, 1.2 hours of an average 48-hour work week). Unfortunately, however, the NSF survey focused on the average number of hours per week devoted to various faculty activities during a 12-month period but did not examine the incidence of such activities.

The two most recent studies of faculty consulting (Boyer 1984; Boyer and Lewis 1984) examined data that were collected by the National Research Council in 1981. Analyses of two stratified subsamples of these NRC data indicate that only 17 to 19 percent of all science, engineering, and humanities faculty reported devoting some portion of their professional work time during the nine-month *academic year* to faculty consulting activities—paid or unpaid. These results are consistent with those of an earlier case study (Counelis 1974), where 15 percent of some 200 faculty at a single institution reported *academic-year* consulting activities (paid and unpaid). These results are surprisingly low, however, when compared directly with results as high as 37 to 54 percent from the previous studies by Patton (1980), Marsh and Dillon (1980), and Lanning (1977). (It is important to note again that the data examined in these studies did not differentiate paid from unpaid consulting. Consequently, none of these studies provide useful information about the extent of paid versus unpaid consulting. Nonetheless, because the studies that did examine paid consulting yielded similar findings to those that examined paid or unpaid consulting, it is likely that the vast majority of consulting examined in these studies was in fact paid consulting.)

Why the apparent discrepancy in results?

One plausible explanation is that all previous studies examined data that included faculty in both professional and nonprofessional fields, whereas the two most recent studies (Boyer 1984; Boyer and Lewis 1984) examined data that did not include doctorate recipients in some professional fields, such as business and education. To the extent that faculty in these professional fields engage in and would report even greater consulting activity, the results of the two most recent studies are underestimated.

Since the several studies of faculty consulting were based, however, on variously defined samples of larger survey data bases, at least some of the discrepancy in results could be attributed to differences among samples. For example, faculty employed in junior colleges were excluded in four studies (Boyer 1984; Boyer and Lewis 1984; Lanning 1977; Marsh and Dillon 1980) but not in the set of studies by Patton and Marver (1976, 1979, 1980), where 60 percent of the faculty who consult were employed in universities, with the balance employed in four-year colleges and junior colleges.

Still another, and the most likely, explanation for the apparent discrepancy in results is that all previous studies sampled over 12- and even 24-month periods that obviously included summers, whereas the two most recent studies (Boyer 1984; Boyer and Lewis 1984) sampled only academic-year activity by asking faculty to describe their activities for the month of February. In the latter studies, the researchers assumed that most consulting contracts span about one-half of the academic year, which appears to be consistent with the assumption that "paid consultation is more regular and of longer duration" than unpaid consultation (Marver and Patton 1976, p. 322). Because February occurs in the middle of the academic year (or at least in the middle of the second academic quarter), it follows that faculty who do any consulting at all during the academic year would be likely to report some consulting activity for the month of February. Given this assumption, the NRC data examined in the two most recent studies are probably more representative of academic-year activity than the data examined in previous studies. Moreover, in light of the earlier assertion that the primary concern of most observers is the alleged double dipping (earning supplemental income on university time) that results from faculty consulting, the NRC data also may be more relevant for purposes of developing institutional policy regarding faculty activities that take place during the academic year.

At the very least, then, the 37 percent incidence reported by Patton (1980) is more likely to represent faculty consulting activity during the total year than the overall incidence reported by Marsh and Dillon (1980) or by Lanning (1977). In turn, the 15 to 19 percent incidence (Boyer 1984; Boyer and Lewis 1984; Counelis 1974) is more likely to represent consulting activity during the academic year.

Is the overall incidence of faculty consulting increasing?

Three studies of faculty consulting examined this question directly (Boyer and Lewis 1984; Dillon 1979b; Patton and Marver 1979). The results of the most recent study (Boyer and Lewis 1984) indicated that, contrary to conventional wisdom, faculty increased their consulting activities only in minor ways from 1975 to 1981; the proportion of science and engineering faculty who reported devoting some portion of their professional work time to consulting increased only from 19 percent in 1975 to 21 percent in 1981. Further, the proportion of faculty who reported devoting more than one day per week to consulting increased less than 0.5 percent from 1975 to 1981. These results substantiate and extend the findings of an earlier study (Patton and Marver 1979), namely, that the proportion of faculty who consult for pay did not change between 1969 and 1975. Only one study (Dillon 1979b) inferred substantial increases in faculty consulting activity. In 1962, 13 percent of all nine-month faculty and 16 percent of all 12-month faculty reported being paid for consulting at least once over a 12-month period (Dunham, Wright, and Chandler 1966), whereas in 1975, 48 percent of all faculty received consulting fees sometime during the preceding two years (Dillon 1979b).

What is the overall extent of faculty consulting?

The results of the most recent study of faculty consulting (Boyer 1984) show that those faculty who do consult (that is, 17.5 percent of the NRC sample) reported devoting a mean of only 11 percent of their professional work time to consulting, although the range was from 1 to 75 percent. Moreover, only one-fourth of those faculty reported devoting more than one day per seven-day week to consulting. Similarly, in another recent national survey of full-time university faculty who consult and whose areas of expertise lie in the professional fields of management, organizational development, organizational communication, or industrial/organizational psychology, less than 20 percent reported devoting the equivalent of more than one day per week to consulting (Glauser and Axley 1983). The latter is surprisingly low when compared with the more broadly based NRC results just presented (Boyer 1984). One would expect university faculty in the professional fields to be among the most active consultants.

Finally, of all faculty in the NRC sample, which included faculty who consult and those who do not, only about 4 percent reported devoting the equivalent of more than one day per calendar week to consulting (Boyer 1984). The latter finding is similar to the 6 percent reported in the only other large-scale study that addressed this question (Patton 1980).

Contrary to conventional wisdom, faculty increased their consulting activities only in minor ways from 1975 to 1981.

What are the characteristics of faculty who consult?

The available evidence suggests that, compared to their faculty colleagues who do not consult, faculty who consult for pay are more likely to be employed in universities than in four-year colleges, whereas faculty who do consult but not for pay are more likely to be employed in two- or four-year institutions than in universities (Bayer 1973; Boyer 1984; Patton 1980; Patton and Marver 1979). Moreover, faculty who are employed in prestigious research universities are more likely to have served as consultants to federal government agencies, national corporations, and foundations (Lipset 1982; Parsons and Platt 1968), whereas faculty employed in two- and four-year colleges are more likely to have served as consultants to local government and business (Patton 1980; Patton and Marver 1979).

In the social sciences and the humanities, full professors are more likely than either associate or assistant professors to engage in consulting and to devote a greater proportion of their professional work time to such outside activities, whereas in fields allied with science and engineering, associate professors are more likely than full or assistant professors to do so (Boyer 1984). In professional fields such as medicine, business, and law, faculty who are politically conservative and higher in academic rank tend to be the most involved in outside consulting (Lanning 1977; Lanning and Blackburn 1979; Marver and Patton 1976; Patton 1980).

Are faculty who consult shirking their other responsibilities?
The available evidence suggests that faculty who consult are at least as active in their other faculty roles as their peers who do not consult. For example, faculty who consult teach as many courses and report devoting as much of their professional work time to teaching and research as their peers who do not consult (Boyer 1984); they also claim to pay more attention to issues of national interest (Boyer and Lewis 1984). Moreover, the more faculty publish, the more likely they are to consult (Fulton and Trow 1974). Thus, "the achievers in academe" not only publish more than their faculty colleagues in major research universities but also are more likely to have served as consultants (Lipset 1982).

With the exception of those faculty who are highly active consultants (Lanning 1977; Lanning and Blackburn 1979), faculty who consult not only teach nearly as much as and publish more than their peers who do not consult, but they also subscribe to more professional journals, communicate more with their colleagues at other institutions, are more satisfied with their careers and their universities, and are at least as active—and/or influential—in departmental and institutional governance (Lanning 1977; Lanning and Blackburn 1979; Marsh and Dillon 1980; Marver and Patton 1976; Patton 1980; Patton and Marver 1979).

Faculty who consult for pay also are "at least as active in their [other] college and university roles" as their peers who do not consult for pay (Patton 1980, p. 184). Apparently, activities producing supplemental income tend not to interfere with other activities traditionally expected of faculty. Even faculty who earn more supplemental income than their peers are more active in research (for example, publish more articles) and are no less active in regular on-campus activities, such as teaching (Marsh and Dillon 1980).

In short, the evidence on faculty consulting is consistent with and extends that of other studies dealing with other forms of faculty activity: "The notion that research involvement detracts from good teaching by channeling professorial time and effort away from the classroom" is "resoundingly disconfirmed" (Finkelstein 1978, pp. 288–89). Similarly, the evidence clearly suggests that, like those faculty who are productive researchers, faculty who consult do so *not* at the expense of their other faculty responsibilities; rather, they represent yet another example of the principle, "the more, the more," that was introduced in Fulton and Trow's well-known study of faculty research activity (1974).

EMPIRICAL RESEARCH ON FACULTY SALARIES AND REPORTED SUPPLEMENTAL INCOME

Questions and issues regarding faculty salaries and reported supplemental income are very much a part of the ongoing debate and policy concerns about faculty consulting. Often at the forefront of this debate are two questions: first, whether faculty are motivated to consult primarily for economic reasons; and second, whether individual faculty members are exploiting their consulting opportunities to increase substantially their total earnings. To address these questions, this section reviews data on the economic status of college and university faculty, reports the current economic position of the academic profession, compares faculty salaries to those of other similar professional groups, and examines the amount and kinds of supplemental income earned by faculty from both "overload" (that is, inside the institution) and outside the institution.

In this latter regard, one must recognize that supplemental income (that is, professional earnings beyond the terms of a regular nine- or 11-month employment contract) for faculty in higher education is not synonymous with double dipping. For example, among the sources of supplemental income for most nine-month faculty are summer earnings from teaching, research, and service within the academic institution and summer earnings from other outside agencies. Supplemental income derived from these and other sources during periods not covered by the regular employment contract is not and should not be considered double dipping. Similarly, given the definition and institutional role for faculty consulting used in this report, one could also argue that supplemental income derived from outside professional consulting that does not interfere with regular faculty responsibilities also should not be considered double dipping.

Sources of Available Data
Several organizations regularly collect and disseminate information on the economic status of college and university faculty. Each year, for example, Committee Z of the American Association of University Professors (AAUP) publishes in *Academe* its "Annual Report on the Economic Status of the Profession." Since 1980, data for these reports have been collected by the National Center for Educational Statistics (NCES) and analyzed for the AAUP

by Maryse Eymonerie Associates. Institutional data are reported for more than 2,000 institutions on average faculty salary, average compensation (average salary plus average fringe benefits), and fringe benefits as a percentage of average salary. The annual reports include data on percentage increases in salary, numbers of full-time faculty, and percentage of tenured faculty. Summary data also are reported by type of institution, type of affiliation (public, private/independent, and church-related), discipline or field of study, sex, tenure status, and academic rank. Trends in the Consumer Price Index (CPI) are compared to trends in average faculty salary, both in monetary and real terms, and the salaries and total money earnings for faculty members and those for other, selected professional groups are compared.

The *Chronicle of Higher Education* is another useful source of data and commentary on the economic status of college and university faculty members. Each year, for example, the *Chronicle* publishes the AAUP's listing of average faculty salaries by rank for more than 2,000 institutions as well as the AAUP summary data on average faculty salaries by rank and type of institution. Each year, the *Chronicle* also publishes salary data collected by the NCES and analyzed for the *Chronicle* by John Minter Associates, a research firm in Boulder, Colorado. Average salary data are reported by rank and sex for more than 1,900 colleges and universities; summary data include statewide and national averages by rank and sex. Until recently, the *Chronicle* also published data collected and analyzed by John Minter Associates regarding extra income earned by faculty members (both within and without their academic institutions).

The NCES is a primary source of data on all levels of education, including higher education. Each year, for example, NCES also publishes its *Digest of Education Statistics,* which includes the latest available statistics from the Higher Education General Information Survey (HEGIS), which NCES conducts annually. Each year, NCES also publishes a statistical report titled *Faculty Salaries, Tenure, and Benefits* that includes current salary data on full-time faculty in both two-year and four-year public and private institutions. Summary data include statewide and regional averages.

The National Research Council is another useful source of data on the demographic characteristics and employment status of doctorate recipients, including those employed full time as faculty in universities or four-year colleges. Its *Survey of Doctorate Recipients* is a large-scale, longitudinal survey of Ph.D.s in the sciences, engineering, and humanities who have earned their degrees since 1930. The survey is conducted biennially with the support of the National Science Foundation, the National Endowment for the Humanities, the National Institutes of Health, and the Department of Energy. Employment data include both base annual salaries and gross professional income. Until recently, the National Science Foundation also conducted its own survey that included salary data (see, for example, NSF 1977).

In addition to these sources of recurrent data on the economic status of college and university faculty, a number of other agencies and scholars also have periodically addressed this issue (see, for example, Bokelman, D'Amico, and Holbrook 1962; Bowen 1978; Brown 1967; Bureau of the Census 1973; Bureau of Labor Statistics 1960 and thereafter; Cartter 1976; Dunham, Wright, and Chandler 1966; Hansen 1979; National Education Association biennial reports; Scientific Manpower Commission 1964, 1971, 1977; Stigler 1950; Tickton 1961; Trivett 1978).

Empirical Research

A reason frequently cited for the alleged increases in paid consulting is the declining economic position of the academic profession over the past decade or so. From 1972–73 to 1983–84, for example, real faculty salaries in the United States declined by almost 20 percent, to 80 percent of their 1972–73 level, with most of that decline occurring between 1975–76 and 1980–81 (AAUP 1981, 1984). In addition, real income for faculty members has recently declined relative to that for other professional and administrative workers (Hansen 1979).

*What is the current economic position
of the academic profession?*

The most recent "Annual Report on the Economic Status
of the Profession" indicates that for 1983–84 "average faculty salary levels expressed in real terms remained roughly
constant, increasing by less than 1 percent" over the preceding year (Hansen 1984, p. 3). Although real faculty salaries had increased for the third consecutive year, the
cumulative total increase for the three-year period was a
modest 3.2 percent (p. 5). In the same three-year period,
the average increase in monetary salary for faculty (all
ranks combined) dropped from 9.0 percent in 1981–82 to
4.7 percent in 1983–84, while the increase in the Consumer
Price Index dropped from 8.7 percent in 1981–82 to an estimated 3.8 percent in 1983–84. Table 1 compares percentage increases in the CPI and in average salary levels, both
monetary and real (all ranks combined), for institutions
reporting comparable data for each of the one-year periods
since 1972–73.

TABLE 1
PERCENTAGE INCREASES IN THE CONSUMER PRICE
INDEX AND AVERAGE SALARY LEVELS, MONETARY
AND REAL[a] (ALL RANKS COMBINED)

Period	Increase in Monetary Salary	Increase in Real Terms	Increase in CPI
1972–73 to 1973–74	5.1	−3.6	9.0
1973–74 to 1974–75	5.8	−4.8	11.1
1974–75 to 1975–76	6.0	−1.0	7.1
1975–76 to 1976–77	4.7	−1.0	5.8
1976–77 to 1977–78	5.3	−1.3	6.7
1977–78 to 1978–79	6.0	−3.1	9.4
1978–79 to 1979–80	7.1	−5.5	13.3
1979–80 to 1980–81	8.7	−2.6	11.6
1980–81 to 1981–82	9.0	0.3	8.7
1981–82 to 1982–83	6.4	2.0	4.3
1982–83 to 1983–84	4.7	0.9	3.8[b]

[a]Monetary salary is salary measured in current dollars. The percentage
increase in real terms is the percentage increase in monetary terms
adjusted for the percentage increase in the Consumer Price Index (on a
standard academic-year basis).
[b]The changes in the CPI for May and June 1984 have been estimated.

Source: AAUP 1984, table 1.

As usual, with an average increase in monetary salary of 5.7 percent, the percentage increase for "continuing" faculty members—that is, those on the same payroll for 1982–83 and 1983–84—exceeded the percentage increases in average salary levels (all ranks and institutions combined).

TABLE 2
PERCENTAGE INCREASES IN MONETARY SALARY LEVELS FOR INSTITUTIONS REPORTING COMPARABLE DATA FOR 1982–83 AND 1983–84

Academic Rank	All Faculty[a]	Continuing Faculty[b]
Public		
Professor	3.9	4.7
Associate	3.8	5.1
Assistant	4.5	5.4
Instructor	5.0	5.2
All Ranks	4.0	5.0
Private Independent		
Professor	6.7	7.3
Associate	6.1	7.6
Assistant	6.5	8.5
Instructor	5.8	7.9
All Ranks	6.5	7.6
Church-related		
Professor	5.8	6.1
Associate	5.6	6.5
Assistant	5.9	7.0
Instructor	5.0	6.7
All Ranks	5.7	6.5
All Combined		
Professor	4.6	5.4
Associate	4.4	5.7
Assistant	5.0	6.3
Instructor	5.1	5.9
All Ranks	4.7	5.7

[a]Sample includes 1,907 institutions reporting comparable data for both years.
[b]Sample includes 1,248 institutions reporting data on continuing faculty (faculty on staff for both 1982–83 and 1983–84).

Source: AAUP 1984, tables 1 and 3.

TABLE 3
AVERAGE MONETARY ACADEMIC-YEAR SALARIES, 1983–84[a]

Academic Rank	All Combined	Public	Private Independent	Church-Related
Category I (Doctoral-level Institutions)				
Professor	41,350	39,770	47,070	41,660
Associate	30,050	29,470	32,430	31,210
Assistant	24,750	24,290	26,380	25,350
Instructor	18,790	18,220	20,940	21,720
Lecturer	21,360	21,300	21,710	20,680
All Ranks	32,650	31,660	36,730	32,140
Category IIA (Comprehensive Institutions)				
Professor	34,750	34,560	36,000	34,790
Associate	27,830	27,770	28,330	27,630
Assistant	23,010	23,040	22,900	22,910
Instructor	18,880	19,110	17,970	18,020
Lecturer	19,370	18,940	20,600	21,760
All Ranks	28,090	28,160	28,080	27,520
Category IIB (General Baccalaureate Institutions)				
Professor	30,860	31,640	34,140	27,920
Associate	25,000	26,270	26,560	23,160
Assistant	20,770	22,230	21,300	19,400
Instructor	17,440	18,570	18,260	16,240
Lecturer	20,050	20,470	21,270	15,870
All Ranks	24,240	25,140	26,250	22,300

Category IIC (Specialized Institutions)

Professor	34,240	40,300	33,710	24,660
Associate	28,150	30,760	27,890	21,670
Assistant	23,460	25,890	23,390	18,350
Instructor	18,660	20,190	18,790	15,480
Lecturer	21,760	22,860	19,380	17,860
All Ranks	27,500	31,660	26,310	21,460

Category III (Two-year Institutions with Academic Ranks)

Professor	31,100	31,510	22,360	21,260
Associate	26,570	26,930	19,730	19,380
Assistant	22,430	22,820	17,110	17,880
Instructor	19,510	20,160	13,990	14,320
Lecturer	15,710	16,100	*	–
All Ranks	24,810	25,340	17,190	17,870

Category IV (Two-year Institutions without Academic Ranks)

No Rank	24,050	24,430	17,990	15,740

All Categories Combined Except IV

Professor	37,400	37,100	41,500	31,340
Associate	28,220	28,430	29,370	25,370
Assistant	23,210	23,540	23,720	20,900
Instructor	18,660	19,140	18,390	16,710
Lecturer	20,710	20,640	21,250	19,430
All Ranks	29,130	29,350	31,080	24,730

[a]Sample includes 2,167 institutions.

Source: AAUP 1984, table 5.

Table 2 shows percentage increases in average monetary salary levels for institutions reporting comparable data for 1982–83 and 1983–84 and for "continuing faculty" by type of institutional affiliation and academic rank, and table 3 presents average monetary academic year salaries for 1983–84, by category, type of institutional affiliation, and academic rank.

As shown in table 3, the 1983–84 average academic-year salary for faculty in major research universities (Category I) ranged from $18,790 for instructors to $41,350 for full professors; the average salary for all ranks combined in that category was $32,650. For all categories combined (except Category IV, where standard academic ranks are not used), the 1983–84 average salary for faculty ranged from $18,660 for instructors to $37,400 for full professors.

How have faculty salaries fared compared to the salaries of other professional groups?

A study of long-term trends in academic salaries and compensation concluded that, in the period since 1970, "compensation in higher education, though it has nearly kept up with the cost of living, has clearly failed to keep pace with compensation in the rest of the economy" (Bowen 1978, p. 10). In the past decade, "faculty members have borne more than their fair share of reduced salary gains" (Hansen 1979, p. 6).

The most recent "Annual Report on the Economic Status of the Profession" compares 1982–83 average academic salary levels with 1982 average salaries of similar professional groups and indicates that faculty salary levels continue to "rank well down in the array" (Hansen 1984, p. 6) (see table 4). The AAUP report for 1983–84 also compares what has happened to real average salaries for selected professional, administrative, and technical positions in private industry to what has happened to real average salaries for faculty in colleges and universities over the past two decades (Hansen 1984). Real average salaries in private industry decreased slightly in the 10 years from 1973 to 1983 but increased by almost 13 percent over the 20 years from 1963 to 1983. By contrast, real average salaries for faculty (all ranks combined) dropped by almost 20 percent

TABLE 4
COMPARISONS OF 1982–83 AVERAGE ACADEMIC-YEAR SALARY LEVELS WITH 1982 AVERAGE ANNUAL SALARIES OF SIMILAR GROUPS OF WORKERS

Salary Range	Federal Government[a] March 1983	Private Industry[a] March 1983	Faculty[b] (All Institutions Combined) Academic Year 1982–83
$85,000		$84,920 (Atty. VI)	
75,000		67,920 (Ch. Acct. IV)	
65,000	$56,310 (GS-15)	66,940 (Engr. VIII)	
55,000		60,470 (Chem. VII)	
		53,180 (Atty. IV)	
		51,460 (Engr. VI)	
		51,300 (Dir. Pers. III)	
45,000	40,320 (GS-13)	42,890 (Chem. V)	
35,000		35,570 (Buyer IV)	$35,470 (Full Professors)
		34,240 (Acct. IV)	
		33,080 (Job Anal. IV)	
25,000	27,720 (GS-11)		27,430 (All Ranks)
			26,840 (Associate Professors)
			21,950 (Assistant Professors)
15,000			17,640 (Instructors)

[a] Bureau of Labor Statistics, September 1983, table D-1. Figures are average annual salaries.
[b] AAUP 1983, table 5. Figures are reported on a standard academic-year basis.

Source: AAUP 1984, table II.

over the same 10-year period and "just held their own" over the 20 years from 1963 to 1983 (p. 7).

When the previous two sets of information are combined, "in real terms average faculty salaries fell relative to private industry salaries by over 16 percent in the 1972–73 to 1982–83 period and by only a slightly smaller amount (10 percent) over the 1962–63 to 1982–83 period" (Hansen 1984, p. 7). Only in one five-year period, 1963 to 1968, when "the tidal wave of baby-boom youth" entered college did average faculty salary increases exceed those in the private sector.

How much supplemental income do faculty earn?
According to a 1980–81 *Chronicle* survey conducted by John Minter Associates, supplemental income averaged $5,756 or 24 percent of the base salaries for 81 percent of all faculty who reported having such extra earnings in 1980–81. This reported supplemental income included extra income from both within and without the institution. According to the same survey, reported outside income averaged $3,873 or 16 percent of base salary (*Chronicle of Higher Education* 1981, pp. 14–15). (It is important to note that these averages were compiled only for those faculty who reported having extra incomes.) Sources of outside income included "research and teaching at other institutions and . . . consulting or other [professional] services." (Royalties, investment income, rents, and gifts were not included.) These results are generally consistent with those reported in five other studies. An early study (Dunham, Wright, and Chandler 1966, pp. 145–49) found that outside earnings in 1962 amounted to 19 percent of base salaries for those on nine- to 10-month appointments and 11 percent for those on 11- to 12-month appointments. In a study based on data from the 1975 Ladd and Lipset survey, reported supplemental earnings for all faculty averaged $2,700, or about 15 percent of base salary (Dillon and Linnell 1980b; Marsh and Dillon 1980). Consulting, as might be expected, was one of two main sources of reported supplemental earnings. In another study that was based on comparable data collected two years later, reported supplemental income still averaged about 15 percent of base salary (Ladd 1978), and in still another, more recent set of

studies that was based on data collected in 1981 by the National Research Council, reported supplemental income for science, engineering, and humanities faculty averaged $3,200 or, again, about 14 percent of base academic salary (Boyer and Lewis 1984).

It is important to note again, however, that all supplemental income does not come solely from consulting but results from all forms of outside professional activity, including teaching and research during the summer months. In another recent study (Anderson 1983), for example, approximately half of some 4,800 faculty in 89 colleges and universities (both public and private) reported having received "no significant outside income." Of those 2,400 faculty who reported sources of outside income, 24 percent identified consulting as their primary source of outside income, another 28 percent noted that their outside income came primarily from work that was "not directly related" to their academic work, and 22 percent said their outside income came primarily from "book royalties and patent income" or "private professional practice"; the remaining 26 percent cited "teaching at other institutions or research" as their primary source of outside income (Anderson 1983, p. 100). Clearly, the latter activities can and should be perceived as natural extensions of normal, on-campus faculty responsibilities and should not be confused with "outside professional consulting."

In an analysis of the 1979 NSF survey data when instructional activities were excluded, faculty devoted only approximately 8 percent of their professional work time to earning outside income. Authoring publications for compensation consumed one-half of the approximately four hours spent per week in earning outside income, while consulting accounted for another one-third of such activities (Lacy and others 1981).

With regard to income derived from consulting, it is important to note that reported supplemental income averaged $2,400 in 1981 or almost 10 percent of base academic salary for those faculty who reported *no* academic-year consulting activity, as compared to $6,600 or approximately 25 percent of base academic salary for those faculty who reported devoting some portion of their professional work time to consulting (Boyer and Lewis 1984). Reported

. . . Faculty devoted only approximately 8 percent of their professional work time to earning outside income.

supplemental income for faculty who did *not* consult averaged between $1,700 (approximately 7 percent of base academic salary) for humanities faculty and $2,800 (approximately 10 percent of base academic salary) for science and engineering faculty (Boyer and Lewis 1984). This supplemental income for those faculty who reported no consulting activity presumably came from overload teaching during the academic year or from teaching, research, and consulting activities during the summer months. Therefore, compared to the overall average of 14 to 16 percent of base academic salary reported in the latter and other studies for both faculty who consult and those who do not (*Chronicle of Higher Education* 1981; Ladd 1978; Marsh and Dillon 1980), the 1981 NRC data suggest that on average, at the most, less than half of all supplemental income can be attributed to outside professional consulting during the academic year (Boyer and Lewis 1984).

Moreover, the 1981 NRC data indicate that less than 10 percent of the science and engineering faculty and less than 4 percent of the humanities faculty reported earning more than $9,000 in supplemental income that, in turn, represented on average only about one-third of their base academic salaries (Boyer and Lewis 1984). In short, it seems reasonable to assume that, on average, faculty are not earning large amounts of supplemental income from consulting or other outside professional activities—and certainly nowhere near the values inferred by some critics of faculty consulting (Linnell 1982).

It is important to point out, however, that reported base academic salary and supplemental income are not distributed evenly across academic disciplines or fields of study. In 1981, for example, supplemental income accounted for a much larger proportion of base academic salary for science and engineering faculty than it did for humanities faculty. Consistent with these results is the market-demand observation (Boyer and Lewis 1984) that the 1981 median annual salary for science and engineering faculty ($31,100) was significantly lower than for their cohort in business/industry ($40,300) or the federal government ($40,400). On the other hand, the 1981 median annual salary for humanities faculty ($26,500) was substantially higher than for their cohort in business and industry ($21,800) but only slightly higher than for their cohort in government ($25,400). (For detailed comparisons of median annual salaries by type of employer, years since completing the Ph.D., and field of doctorate, see tables 5 and 6.)

Are total faculty earnings competitive when supplemental income is taken into account?

Even though faculty salaries have fallen relative to the salaries for their cohorts in similar professional groups, some reviewers argue that faculty salaries still compare favorably when all forms of supplemental income and summer earnings are taken into account. "The augmentation of compensation by substantial nonmonetary benefits and outside income places faculty in a strong position relative to comparable workers in other industries" (Bowen 1978, p. 13). When both nonmonetary benefits and outside income averaging 11 to 15 percent of base salary are taken into account, faculty on 11- to 12-month appointments actually may be better off than their cohorts in business and government. Marsh and Dillon (1980) came to similar conclusions when they compared total earnings of 16 professional groups, as reported by the Bureau of the Census, and found that faculty salaries ranked near the midpoint of these groups. On the basis of such findings, they argued, "academic salaries were not grossly out of line with those of other highly educated professional groups" (p. 554). Nonetheless, if one compares the *annualized* median salaries that are based upon data from the National Research Council (see tables 5 and 6), it does appear that the salaries for Ph.D. faculty in fields allied with science and engineering are substantially below those for their cohorts in business, industry, and the federal government. On the other hand, Ph.D. faculty in the humanities appear to be relatively better off by being employed in educational institutions.

Comparisons of faculty earnings are not always based on comparable data. For example, all salary data reported by the AAUP in conjunction with Maryse Eymonerie Associates and the NCES reflect average base salaries by rank reported on a nine-month basis, with 12-month earnings converted to their proportional nine-month equivalents. Thus, when faculty earnings are compared to those of

TABLE 5
MEDIAN ANNUAL SALARIES OF FULL-TIME EMPLOYED DOCTORAL SCIENTISTS AND ENGINEERS, 1981

Years since Ph.D.	All Fields	Math	Computer Sci.	Physics/ Astron.	Chem.	Environ. Earth	Engrg.	Agric.	Med.	Biol.	Psych.	Social Sci.
						Field of Doctorate (thousands of dollars)						
Total	$34.8	$31.8	$34.8	$36.9	$36.9	$34.9	$40.2	$33.1	$36.5	$32.5	$30.9	$30.9
5 or less	26.6	23.9	32.3	29.6	29.6	28.0	33.0	25.4	28.4	23.9	24.0	24.3
6–10	31.3	29.1	36.8	34.6	33.5	32.6	37.9	30.4	35.1	28.1	28.4	29.2
11–15	36.5	32.9		37.1	37.0	38.6	42.5	35.1	38.8	33.8	33.9	35.0
16–20	39.6	37.2			40.7	39.7	45.3	37.3	47.9	37.3	36.6	37.1
21–25	41.9	41.9		43.7	40.9		48.4	38.2	46.0	39.8	40.7	39.5
26–30	45.5			48.4	45.9		50.2	40.9	46.0	44.0	42.9	44.0
Over 30	46.6	47.2			47.5	50.3	50.3	42.0	50.1	46.0	44.9	44.9

Total	$34.8	$31.8	$34.8	$36.9	$36.9	$34.9	$40.2	$33.1	$36.5	$32.5	$30.9	$30.9
Educational Institution	31.1	30.5	29.5	34.0	31.3	30.5	36.2	31.3	33.5	30.5	29.0	29.8
4-Year College/University/ Medical School	31.3	30.6	29.4	34.2	31.4	30.6	36.2	31.3	33.6	30.6	28.9	29.8
2-Year College	28.2			30.0						25.8	28.0	27.1
Elementary/Secondary School	29.2										30.7	
Business/Industry	40.3	36.4	40.1	39.5	40.3	40.5	41.6	35.4	44.6	38.2	40.3	38.9
U.S. Government, Civilian	40.4	39.3			39.8	40.7	44.2	38.9	39.6	37.6		44.2
State/Local Government	28.9					27.5		30.4			27.9	29.2
Hospital/Clinic	31.1				32.6					35.4	30.1	
Other Nonprofit Organization	35.5	35.7		37.0	37.2	34.7	40.5			33.1	30.5	30.4

Median salaries were computed only for Ph.D.s employed full time, excluding those in the U.S. military. Academic salaries were multiplied by 11/9 to adjust for a full-year scale. Medians were not reported for cells with fewer than 20 cases reporting salary or with a sampling error of more than ± $2,000.

Source: National Research Council 1982, tables 1.7 and 1.8.

TABLE 6
MEDIAN ANNUAL SALARIES OF FULL-TIME EMPLOYED PH.D.S IN THE HUMANITIES, 1981

Field of Doctorate

Years since Ph.D.	All Fields	Hist.	Art Hist.	Music	Speech/ Theater	Phil.	Other Hum.	Eng./ Amer. Lang. & Lit.	Class. Lang. & Lit.	Modern Lang. & Lit.
					(thousands of dollars)					
Total	$26.3	$27.0	$25.2	$26.0	$28.3	$26.0	$27.1	$26.2	$24.9	$25.4
5 or less	20.4	20.2	19.8	21.6	21.2	20.2	21.0	20.9	18.1	19.1
6–10	24.4	24.7	25.2	25.4	26.2	24.2	26.9	24.0	23.0	24.2
11–15	28.9	28.5		30.7	29.2	29.5		29.7	28.0	28.0
16–20	32.7	34.4	34.6	32.0		34.3	38.3	30.9		32.2
21–25	35.1	36.5				33.2		35.2		34.6
26–30	39.2	40.1								
Over 30	40.2									

Total	$26.3	$27.0	$25.2	$26.0	$28.3	$26.0	$27.1	$26.2	$24.9	$25.4
Educational Institution	26.5	27.5	25.4	26.4	28.4	26.5	27.9	26.4	25.4	25.6
4-Year College/University/Medical School	26.5	27.3	25.3	26.4	28.3	26.6	27.9	26.5	25.3	25.5
2-Year College	26.6	29.6						24.1		
Elementary/Secondary School	25.6									24.4
Business/Industry	21.8	18.5				18.5				
Government	25.4	25.5								
Other/No Report	22.3							19.0		

Median salaries were computed only for Ph.D.s employed full time, excluding those in the U.S. military. Academic salaries were multiplied by 11/9 to adjust for a full-year scale. Medians were not reported for cells with fewer than 20 cases reporting salary or a sampling error of ± $2,000.

Source: National Research Council 1982, tables 2.7 and 2.8.

other occupations, the former appear artificially low if and when they exclude supplemental earnings (for example, from summer or overload teaching, research, or administrative assignments, and from consulting or other services). A similar problem arises when faculty earnings are compared across institutions, depending on whether the data reflect average salaries for all faculty members or average salaries for continuing faculty members. Because the latter excludes new hires who most likely would be relatively low paid, its results would tend to overstate both average salaries and percentage increases from one year to the next. In recent years, this problem arose when AAUP/ NCES data were compared with data collected in a survey conducted for the *Chronicle* by John Minter Associates of Boulder, Colorado (see AAUP 1982).

To compare properly faculty salaries as reported by AAUP and the salaries for other similar groups of professional workers, supplemental income earned by faculty must be appropriately adjusted. For example, if the average faculty salary level (all ranks combined) for the 1982–83 academic year (as reported by the AAUP in table 4) is increased by supplemental income averaging 15 percent (as reported in most studies of supplemental income), then the average faculty salary level for all ranks combined would increase from $27,430 to $31,545. The latter figure, however, is still substantially below almost all of the other similar groups of workers identified in table 4.

Are faculty motivated to consult primarily for economic reasons?

In Logan Wilson's ground-breaking inquiry of 1942, low academic salaries were identified as "the origin of conflict between multiple roles," and it was argued that low salaries lead to "diffusion, not to mention dissipation, of energy" in outside activities, such as consulting (1942, pp. 137–38). By linking the pursuit of outside activities to the pursuit of economic self-interest, what Wilson effectively did was to equate "academic man" with "economic man," thereby laying the foundation for much of the current conventional wisdom about faculty consulting. Moreover, Wilson has twice since reinforced the image of "academic man" as "economic man" that was presented in 1942—

once in 1965 and again in 1979. Even in the 1980s, Wilson's image continues to be presented. For example, in a recent book devoted to examining the role of supplemental income and its relationship to faculty ethics (Linnell 1982), the underlying premise is that faculty indeed are induced by external dollars to devote increasing amounts of time and energy to outside professional activities. A second premise of the book is that "outside funding is corrupting to the academic ideal" and that "large amounts of money will surely corrupt more than small amounts" (Tuckman 1984, p. 431).

Nonetheless, and despite the significant decline in real faculty salaries over the past decade, the studies reported in this report suggest that increasing numbers of faculty are *not* being induced to seek outside professional consulting activities to supplement their base academic salaries (Boyer and Lewis 1984; Patton 1980; Patton and Marver 1979), nor are they substantially increasing their supplemental income (Boyer and Lewis 1984; Ladd 1978; Marsh and Dillon 1980). Rather, both the steady proportion of total faculty earnings accounted for by supplemental income and the steady proportion of faculty who consult are consistent with the additional finding that, among such faculty who consult, the percentage of professional work time devoted to consulting is not related to base academic salary (Boyer and Lewis 1984). In fact, faculty who consult on average report higher base academic salaries than their peers who do not consult. These findings are particularly important for two reasons. First, they indicate that the highest paid faculty probably are paid high salaries because they are regarded as high-quality, experienced faculty and because they are employed in market-competitive fields where the demand is high in alternative employment opportunities and for their consulting expertise. Second, these findings challenge much of the current conventional wisdom about faculty consulting. In short, "academic man" is *not* "economic man." Rather, most faculty appear to be motivated primarily by other important factors, such as those identified earlier in this report.

POLICIES AND PRACTICES ON FACULTY CONSULTING AND OTHER SUPPLEMENTAL INCOME ACTIVITIES

It has been generally understood that the policies of most academic institutions permit faculty members to engage in consulting and other activities producing supplemental income so long as such activities do not interfere with their other faculty responsibilities, employ institutional resources, or raise questions about conflict of interest. Only recently, however, have researchers attempted to survey institutions and identify those provisions most commonly included in institutional policies and practices on faculty consulting and other activities producing supplemental income. In the past five years, four such surveys have been reported in the literature (Allard 1982; Dillon and Bane 1980; Teague 1982; Weston 1980–81). With one exception (Allard 1982), these surveys all focus exclusively on policies in major colleges and universities. Nonetheless, the results of these surveys reflect the wide range of institutional approaches being used, from having no formal policy to having a policy that prohibits all outside employment. Similarly, the assumptions underlying these policies range from "what you do on your own time is your business" to "whatever you do is our business and subject to institutional regulation."

In length and detail, the policies examined in the four studies range from statements of general application to lengthy documents accompanied by prescribed forms. Nonetheless, almost every institutional policy examined includes both a statement of the professional commitment to the institution required by a full-time faculty appointment and a stipulation that outside professional activities should not interfere with the performance of one's responsibilities to the institution (Allard 1982; Teague 1982). Moreover, at least among major colleges and universities, the policies in public institutions tend to be more complex and prescriptive than those commonly found in private institutions. Most of the institutions surveyed, however, do not have clearly instructive, detailed policy statements. Yet, as is evident from the survey results, most colleges and universities do monitor the consulting and outside professional activities of their faculty, at least insofar as they maintain some form of policies regarding these matters. This section reviews institutional policies and practices on faculty consulting and other activities producing supplemental income. [For institutions contemplating policy review and revision in these matters, a useful checklist that enumerates, by individual institution, the principal policies of 98 major colleges and universities can be found in Dillon and Bane (1980).]

Policies and Practices at Major Colleges and Universities
A review of the results of the four studies (Allard 1982; Dillon and Bane 1980; Teague 1982; Weston 1980–81) reveals some important similarities among academic institutions in the policies being promulgated, the practices being employed to implement the policies, and the means used to monitor outside professional activities. For example, almost all of the major colleges and universities surveyed in the four studies did have policies governing faculty consulting and other outside professional activities. Moreover, nearly every institutional policy examined in these studies started with an acknowledgment of the benefits of faculty consulting to both the individual faculty member and the academic institution. Table 7 compares the results of two studies (Dillon and Bane 1980; Teague 1982) in terms of provisions commonly included in institutional policies on faculty consulting and other activities producing supplemental income.

In both public and private institutions, most policies have three common components: (1) a description of the activity to be regulated through policy; (2) the limitations on or regulations governing that activity; and (3) the permission needed or procedures to be followed before pursuing the activity.

Description of the activity
Almost without exception, consulting and other outside professional activities are subject to disclosure and/or regulation by the academic institution. Among the policies examined, consulting was generally defined as performing a service in one's profession, field of study, or discipline for an individual or agency outside the university and receiving a fee for that service, although many definitions also included unpaid activities. Interestingly, some institutions excluded from such regulation outside work that was not directly related to the faculty member's profession,

TABLE 7
PROVISIONS COMMONLY INCLUDED IN INSTITUTIONAL POLICIES ON FACULTY CONSULTING AND OTHER SUPPLEMENTAL INCOME ACTIVITIES

	Percent of Institutional Policies Containing Each Provision	
	Teague (1982) N=236	*Dillon and Bane (1980)* N=98
Description of the Activity		
Concern with nonacademic year	17%	25%
Regulations and Limitations		
Conflict of interest	56	25
Time limitations	48	68
Use of materials/facilities	37	52
Use of institutional name	23	33
Concern with compensation	8	17
Procedures and Permission Needed		
Prior approval	61	76
Disclosure/reporting requirement	46	33
Violation of policy	4	10

Source: Dillon and Bane 1980; Teague 1982.

field of study, or discipline (that is, moonlighting, as when an economist takes up farming or a forester sells insurance). On the other hand, more than 10 percent of the institutional policies examined in one study (Dillon and Bane 1980) included restrictions regarding outside professional activities during the nonacademic year and other nonpayroll periods (during summers and leaves of absence, for example), although most of such restrictions related to the use of institutional facilities and the institution's name.

No clear conceptual understanding of what constitutes consulting and other outside professional activities presently exists. Nonetheless, in their attempts to define such activities, some institutions differentiate between so-called "scholarly" and "professional" outside activities simply on the basis of whether the faculty member receives a fee for service. The implication, of course, is that the former somehow have greater imputed value in terms of faculty service and less need for review or oversight. When, however, "scholarly" service is excluded from institutional policies governing consulting activities, such labeling and reasoning seem to imply that "scholars" are expected to take oaths of poverty with regard to public service. If an institution cannot clearly define the outside activities to be regulated, then no matter how explicit the actual limitations on such activities might be, the institutional policy as a whole is likely to be seriously flawed.

Limitations and regulations

Conflict of interest. The issue of conflict of interest was one of the most common concerns reported by the institutions surveyed. It is important to note, however, that only about one-fourth of these policies cited the joint statement on conflict of interest that was developed in 1965 by the American Association of University Professors and the American Council on Education (ACE) (AAUP 1977); the remaining three-fourths merely included a statement of a more general nature granting faculty the privilege of "engaging in nonuniversity outside employment of any kind . . . [provided] that no conflict of interest arises between their obligation to the University and any extra University employment" (Teague 1982, p. 183). Moreover, the policies examined did not always include a description of the procedures for determining whether an actual or potential conflict of interest existed or, for that matter, identify who was responsible for making such a determination. It was suggested that in those institutions that did not require prior approval, such determination apparently resided with the individual faculty member (Teague 1982). Surprisingly, only a few institutions specified under what circumstances teaching could be performed for an outside educational organization.

Time limitations. In most of the institutional policies examined, it was common to limit the amount of time that individual faculty members can devote to consulting and other outside professional activities. In some policies, such limitations were rather loosely defined (for example, consulting activities should not "compromise the effectiveness of the faculty member" or should not "interfere with normal activities" (Weston 1980–81, p. 75). In most policies, however, these limitations were stated far more precisely. As shown in table 7, 50 to 70 percent of the policies examined in the two studies contained provisions setting actual time limitations on outside professional activities. [Similar results have been reported in a recent study of active faculty consultants (Glauser and Axley 1983), where more than 65 percent of the survey respondents said their institution restricted the number of days they could devote to outside consulting activities.] "One day per week" was by far the most common time limitation. But what constitutes a week? In some policies, a week is five days, in others seven days, and in still others, it is undefined. In other policies, this limitation was expressed as "eight hours per week," "four working days per month," "13 days per academic quarter," or "39 days per academic year."

Such specification of time limitations is especially interesting, given the content of the AAUP-ACE policy statement cited earlier. Although the joint statement was developed specifically to address relationships among faculty members, institutions, and government agencies that are peculiar to contract research opportunities, the section on "distribution of effort" is relevant to the present discussion:

> There are competing demands on the energies of a faculty member (for example, research, teaching, committee work, outside consulting). The way in which he divides his effort among these various functions does not raise ethical questions unless the Government agency supporting his research is misled in its understanding of the amount of intellectual effort he is actually devoting to the research in question. A system of precise time accounting is incompatible with the inherent character of the work of a faculty member, since the various functions he performs are closely interrelated and do not

. . . Such labeling and reasoning seem to imply that "scholars" are expected to take oaths of poverty. . . .

conform to any meaningful division of a standard work week (AAUP 1977, p. 82).

Consistent with the intent of this AAUP-ACE statement, a few of the institutions surveyed expressed time limitations in terms of percentages of the individual faculty member's full-time obligation. The latter seems to represent an attempt to measure effort rather than time and certainly is more consistent with generally accepted faculty accounting practices and with recent interpretations by auditors of federal grants and contracts (Weston 1980–81). Also consistent at least with the intent of the AAUP-ACE statement, but less clear for policy purposes, some 30 to 50 percent of the policies examined in the two studies reported in table 7 included no stipulation regarding time limitations, suggesting that it was left to the individual faculty member or perhaps to some administrator (the department head, for example) to determine what constitutes meeting one's other university responsibilities.

Use of institutional materials and facilities. Because institutional materials and facilities are particularly susceptible to abuse by individual faculty members and other university staff, one would expect the use of such materials and facilities to be an important component of institutional policies on faculty consulting and other outside professional activities. Surprisingly, however, as shown in table 7, fewer than half of the policies examined in the two studies included any provisions regarding the use of institutional materials and facilities by faculty in conjunction with their outside professional activities. Those policies that did address this issue either specified constraints on or required reimbursement for the use of such materials and facilities. Many policies also specified that an administrator (from department head to vice president) was authorized to grant permission to use such resources "in highly unusual cases," the principal criterion being whether the outside professional activity would benefit the institution as well as the individual faculty member; all other cases required reimbursement for the use of such materials and facilities. Apparently, however, a number of institutions absolutely prohibited any such use of institutional materials and facilities. If taken literally, it is not clear whether under the latter circumstances an individual faculty member who engaged in some outside professional activity would actually be allowed even to use a personally owned desktop computer in her office, answer an office telephone, or use a pencil or notepad that was furnished by the institution.

Other restrictions. As shown in table 7, use of the institution's name was restricted in approximately one-fourth to one-third of the policies examined. Some institutions stipulate that its name should not be used if such use might imply institutional support for the outside professional activity; others require the individual faculty member to provide the outside agency with a written declaration that the college or university did not support the work. Some institutions actually restricted the amount of compensation that individual faculty members can earn from outside professional activities. As shown in table 7, for example, 8 to 17 percent of the policies examined actually restricted compensation for outside professional activities. It is likely that most such restrictions would apply to faculty in clinical and professional fields, would be stated in terms of percentages of base salary, and would be related to a specific service function of the institution. Generally, however, compensation for outside professional activities was regarded as a matter between the individual faculty member and the outside agency.

Permission required and procedures
Overall, compared with private colleges, the procedures of public colleges and universities tended to have more rigorous requirements regarding prior approval and disclosure of outside professional activities (Weston 1980–81).

Prior approval of outside professional activities. As shown in table 7, approximately 60 to 75 percent of the policies examined included provisions requiring some form of prior approval of consulting and other outside professional activities. More than half of the policies examined in Teague's study specified that such approval must be obtained from the department head and/or dean, although in many institutions individual faculty members did not follow this procedure closely or administrators strictly enforce it. The formality of the procedures for obtaining prior approval varied greatly among the institutions, yet almost all used a standard request form on which the faculty member was asked to provide the name of the outside agency, a description of the type of consulting activity, the dates of such activity, and a list of any institutional facilities to be used.

Regardless of the approval procedure, however, criteria for granting permission were almost nonexistent in many of the policies examined (Teague 1982). The most commonly mentioned factors were amount of time required by the outside professional activity, possible interference with other on-campus responsibilities, and potential contribution to the professional development of the individual faculty member.

Disclosure or reporting requirement. One-third to almost one-half of the institutional policies examined required faculty to "submit an annual written disclosure report" (Dillon and Bane 1980) or had some sort of reporting requirement, although the frequency of such reports ranged from "at time of agreement" to "annually" (Teague 1982). A written report was not, however, often specified and a standard reporting form or format usually not required. Rather, individual faculty members were asked to describe the nature and extent of their outside professional activities and to "inform their supervisor [usually the department head] of all current consulting activities as they occur" (Teague 1982, p. 183).

Surprisingly, only 4 to 10 percent of the policies examined indicated disciplinary actions that could result from violation of such policy. Such a provision is indeed important, as individual faculty members are "entitled to know the possible consequences for improper actions with regard to consulting [and other outside professional] activities" (Teague 1982, p. 185).

Policies and Practices at Four-Year Colleges and Community Colleges
As noted earlier, only one recent study has examined the policies governing outside professional activities at institu-

tions other than major colleges and universities. Allard (1982) examined policies at state universities, at four-year colleges (both public and private), and at community colleges in Maryland and found such policies to be generally consistent with those of some 40 peer institutions across the country, although the details of the policies and the procedures for implementation varied considerably—especially by type of institution. As in the other studies cited earlier (Dillon and Bane 1980; Teague 1982; Weston 1980–81), it was found that state universities generally viewed consulting and other outside professional activities "as an important component of the institution's ability to provide service to the larger society," usually encouraged such activity, and were often permissive in doing so (Allard 1982, p. 15). By comparison, public four-year colleges also generally encouraged faculty to participate in outside professional activities but were somewhat more likely to set specific and tighter limits on the amount of time that could be devoted to such activities, whereas most private liberal arts colleges actually discouraged (and, in one case, prohibited) outside professional employment of faculty.

It is interesting to note that fewer private liberal arts colleges and community colleges had policies governing outside professional activity but that those that did were far more likely to have restrictive policies, especially with regard to amount of compensation, time limitations, and prior approval.

In summary, in many institutions the policies and procedures governing faculty consulting and other activities producing supplemental income often fail to address formally many important considerations. Even in those institutions where the policies are fairly specific with regard to limitations, the procedures for implementing the policies and for monitoring the outside professional activities of individual faculty members often are seriously lacking. On the other hand, in some institutions the policies appear to be unnecessarily restrictive and even unmanageable. In many institutions, therefore, more explicit and carefully developed policies and procedures governing faculty consulting and other supplemental income activities clearly are in order.

SOME CONCLUDING OBSERVATIONS

Beyond the many specific policy implications and research observations already presented in this report, several additional and more general implications emerge for academic policy makers and researchers in higher education.

Implications for Policy and Practice
As a general policy guideline, the literature review in this report indicates that both field of employment and type of institution are important in determining whether and how much faculty consult. Clearly, the finding that faculty employed in universities (and in some fields) are both more in demand and more likely to consult than those employed in four-year colleges (and in other fields) suggests at least that some consideration be given to having different faculty consulting policies for different types of institutions (and perhaps for different fields or units within institutions).

The literature also indicates that faculty who consult, on average, teach as many courses, devote as much of their professional work time to teaching and research, and are at least as active as their peers who do not consult. These findings are especially important because they suggest that, in practice as well as in theory, consulting can be an integral part of overall faculty role.

All of which suggests that in many cases institutional policy governing faculty consulting ought to be revised (or newly created, if necessary) to better accommodate not only type of institution and field of employment but also individual differences in workload and productivity. Moreover, to be truly effective, such policy should allow for individual, case-by-case review when the percentage of time devoted to consulting exceeds a prescribed ceiling (in most institutions, the latter usually is the equivalent of one day per week). (As reported earlier, nearly one-fourth of faculty who consult reported devoting the equivalent of more than one day per week to consulting, although the comparable figure for both faculty who consult and those who do not was only 4 to 6 percent.)

Consider, for example, the case of individual faculty members who are highly productive as scholars and as teachers and who at the same time devote the equivalent of more than one day per week to consulting. It could be argued that those faculty should be not only permitted but encouraged to engage in consulting activities. The same argument could apply to individual faculty members who work, say, 60 or more hours per week to incorporate consulting into their professional work time and still meet their other university responsibilities. Conceivably, then, institutional policy that imposes an upper limit on the percentage of time devoted to consulting (for example, one day per seven-day calendar week) might restrict the overall productivity of highly active faculty—especially those for whom field-based consulting provides an interactive link with, and thereby enhances, research and teaching.

In summary, more explicit guidelines are needed, provided such guidelines are not necessarily more restrictive. To the contrary, the results presented in this report suggest that institutional policy governing faculty consulting should allow for the percentage of time devoted to consulting to vary depending on individual productivity. Clearly, steps should be taken to ensure that such policy does not discriminate against the most highly active and valued faculty.

Directions for Further Research
Further research on faculty consulting and other activities producing supplemental income is needed in at least four important areas.

First, lack of theory on which to base research on faculty activities and evaluate its results has become increasingly problematic as national survey data on consulting and other faculty activities accumulate. As noted earlier, this lack of theory is recognized as a weakness that has kept "the sociology of the academic profession from maturing as a science" (Light 1974, pp. 2–3). Without the explanatory principles supplied by theory, the results of existing studies are at risk for meaningful interpretation and effective integration. National agencies should be encouraged to better coordinate their research efforts and to take seriously a conceptual framework that includes outside professional activities as an integral part of both faculty role and institutional mission. The review of research literature and data on faculty consulting in this report indicates that empirical research is being conducted by agencies such as the National Center for Education Statistics, the National Research Council, and the National Science Foundation but apparently with little, if any, interagency communication or collaboration. Such lack of communication and collaboration limits the utility and comparability of national survey data. At the very least, these national agencies should be encouraged to develop a single sampling scheme for use in research on the full range of faculty activities, including consulting.

Second, the results of the studies reviewed in this report provide a fairly complete picture of the overall incidence and extent of faculty consulting for different time periods (week, month, academic year, and calendar year), yet little is known about individual patterns of faculty consulting over time and careers. In this regard, the importance of asking the most appropriate questions for informing institutional policy cannot be overstated. Further research in this area would contribute importantly to the literature on faculty consulting and career development.

Third, the results of the most recent studies provide a necessary starting point for further research on the opportunity cost of faculty consulting and whether the real opportunity cost is to leisure—and therefore is borne by the individual—or to the institution. Attention should be directed toward developing an economic model that takes into account the various tradeoffs not only among the traditional functions of research, teaching, and service, but also between each of these three functions and a fourth function, leisure. Such a model could be used to address several empirical questions, including what faculty who consult would do with the additional time gained if they did not consult and to what extent faculty value consulting as a professional activity.

Finally, the results presented in this report suggest that additional research needs to be targeted more directly on what faculty allegedly take back to the institution as a result of their consulting activities. How much of what faculty learn while consulting actually informs their instructional activities or influences their research on campus? What is the joint product of consulting, teaching, and research? Especially important in light of recent concerns is the need to understand better the nature and extent to

Institutional policy governing faculty consulting should allow for the percentage of time devoted to consulting to vary depending on individual productivity.

which faculty are influenced in their research priorities and academic objectivity by their outside professional relationships. This latter point is currently almost wholly unexplored in the research literature.

REFERENCES

The ERIC Clearinghouse on Higher Education abstracts and indexes the current literature on higher education for the National Institute of Education's monthly bibliographic journal *Resources in Education*. Most of these publications are available through the ERIC Document Reproduction Service (EDRS). For publications cited in this bibliography that are available from EDRS, ordering number and price are included, Readers who wish to order a publication should write to the ERIC Document Reproduction Service, P.O. Box 190, Arlington, Virginia 22210. When ordering, please specify the document number. Documents are available as noted in microfiche (MF) and paper copy (PC). Because prices are subject to change, it is advisable to check the latest issue of *Resources in Education* for current cost based on the number of pages in the publication.

Aggarwal, Raj. 1981. "Faculty Members as Consultants: A Policy Perspective." *Journal of the College and University Personnel Association* 32(2): 17–20.

Allard, Sandra. August 1982. "A Summary of Institutional Policies Affecting Outside and Offload Employment for Faculty at Maryland Public Higher Education Institutions." Unpublished manuscript, State Board for Higher Education, Annapolis, Md. ED 221 127. 24 pp. MF–$0.97; PC–$3.54.

Altbach, Philip G. 1978. "Studying the Academic Profession." In *Studies on Academics and Modes of Inquiry,* edited by Robert T. Blackburn. Ann Arbor: University of Michigan, Center for the Study of Higher Education. ED 167 062. 99 pp. MF–$0.97; PC–$9.36.

American Association of University Professors. 1977. *AAUP Policy Documents and Reports*. Washington, D.C.: Author. ED 136 646. 105 pp. MF–$0.97; PC–$11.16.

————. 1979. "An Era of Continuing Decline: Annual Report on the Economic Status of the Profession, 1978–79." *Academe: Bulletin of the AAUP* 65(5): 319–30.

————. 1980. "Regressing into the Eighties: Annual Report on the Economic Status of the Profession, 1979–80. *Academe: Bulletin of the AAUP* 66(5): 260–74.

————. 1981. "The Rocky Road through the 1980s: Annual Report on the Economic Status of the Profession, 1980–81." *Academe: Bulletin of the AAUP* 67(4): 210–30.

————. 1982. "Surprises and Uncertainties: Annual Report on the Economic Status of the Profession, 1981–82." *Academe: Bulletin of the AAUP* 68(4): 3–23.

———. 1983. "A Blip on the Screen: Annual Report on the Economic Status of the Profession, 1982–83." *Academe: Bulletin of the AAUP* 69(4): 1–75.

———. 1984. "Bottoming Out? Annual Report on the Economic Status of the Profession, 1983–84." *Academe: Bulletin of the AAUP* 70(2): 2–63.

Anderson, Richard E. 1983. *Finance and Effectiveness: A Study of College Environments*. Princeton, N.J.: Educational Testing Service. ED 242 232. 193 pp. MF–$0.97; PC not available EDRS.

Austin, Ann E., and Gamson, Zelda F. 1983. *Academic Workplace: New Demands, Heightened Tensions*. ASHE-ERIC Higher Education Research Report No. 10. Washington, D.C.: Association for the Study of Higher Education. ED 243 397. 131 pp. MF–$0.97; PC–$12.96.

Axford, Roger W. 1967. *College-Community Consultation*. DeKalb, Ill.: Enlightenment Press. ED 012 874. 48 pp. MF–$0.97; PC–$5.34.

Baldwin, Roger G., and Blackburn, Robert T. 1981. "The Academic Career as a Developmental Process: Implications for Higher Education." *Journal of Higher Education* 52(6): 598–614.

Bayer, Alan E. 1973. *Teaching Faculty in Academe: 1972–73*. ACE Research Reports 8(2). Washington, D.C.: American Council on Education. ED 080 517. 65 pp. MF–$0.97; PC–$7.14.

Blackburn, Robert T. 1974. "The Meaning of Work in Academia." In *Assessing Faculty Effort,* edited by James I. Doi. New Directions for Institutional Research No. 2. San Francisco: Jossey-Bass.

———. 1978. "Case Studies of the Academic Profession." In *Studies on Academics and Modes of Inquiry,* edited by Robert T. Blackburn. Ann Arbor: University of Michigan, Center for the Study of Higher Education. ED 167 062. 99 pp. MF–$0.97; PC–$9.36.

Bok, Derek. 1982. *Beyond the Ivory Tower: Social Responsibilities of the Modern University*. Cambridge, Mass.: Harvard University Press.

Bokelman, W. Robert; D'Amico, Louis A.; and Holbrook, Anna Jane. 1962. *A Half Century of Salaries at Land-Grant Institutions*. Washington, D.C.: U.S. Office of Education, Department of Health, Education, and Welfare (OE-52004-3).

Bowen, Howard R. 1977. *Investment in Learning: The Individual and Social Value of American Higher Education*. San Francisco: Jossey-Bass.

————. 1978. *Academic Compensation: Are Faculty and Staff in American Higher Education Adequately Paid?* New York: Teachers Insurance and Equity Association, College Retirement Equities Fund. ED 155 994. 139 pp. MF–$0.97; PC–$12.96.

Boyer, Carol M. 1984. "Faculty Consulting: Salient Issues, Correlates, and Policy Implications." Ph.D. dissertation, University of Minnesota.

Boyer, Carol M., and Lewis, Darrell R. 1984. "Faculty Consulting: Responsibility or Promiscuity?" *Journal of Higher Education* 55(5): 637–59.

Brown, David G. 1967. *The Mobile Professors.* Washington, D.C.: American Council on Education.

Bureau of the Census. 1973. *Earnings by Occupation and Education.* Special Report PC(2)-8B, U.S. Department of Commerce, 1970. Washington, D.C.: U.S. Government Printing Office.

Bureau of Labor Statistics, U.S. Department of Labor. 1960 and thereafter. *National Survey of Professional, Administrative, Technical, and Clerical Pay.* Washington, D.C.: U.S. Government Printing Office.

Caplow, Theodore, and McGee, Reece J. 1958. *The Academic Marketplace.* New York: Basic Books.

Cartter, Allan M. 1976. *Ph.D.s and the Academic Labor Market.* New York: McGraw-Hill.

Cheit, Earl F. 1975. *The Useful Arts and the Liberal Tradition.* New York: McGraw-Hill.

Chronicle of Higher Education. 9 December 1981. "Estimated Earnings of Faculty Members beyond Their Basic Salaries for 1980–81" 23(15): 14.

Cilley, Earl G. L. 1977. "Faculty Consulting: Issues in Academic Policy Development." Paper presented at Second Annual Academic Planning Conference, University of Southern California, January, Los Angeles. ED 138 172. 13 pp. MF–$0.97; PC–$3.54.

Clark, Burton R. 1978. "The Academic Profession: New Directions of Research." In *Studies on Academics and Modes of Inquiry,* edited by Robert T. Blackburn. Ann Arbor: University of Michigan, Center for the Study of Higher Education. ED 167 062. 99 pp. MF–$0.97; PC–$9.36.

Clark, Henry. 1978. "The Professional Vocation: A Modest Proposal." Paper presented at the Third Annual Academic Planning Conference, University of Southern California, January, Los Angeles. ED 152 194. 15 pp. MF–$0.97; PC–$3.54.

Clark, Henry B., and Dillon, Kristine E. 1982. "The Ethics of the Academic Profession." In *Dollars and Scholars: An Inquiry into the Impact of Faculty Income upon the Function and Future of the Academy,* edited by Robert H. Linnell. Los Angeles: University of Southern California Press.

Clark, Shirley M. 1983. "Qualitative Approaches to the Study of Faculty Career Vitality: Problems and Contributions." Paper presented at the annual meeting of the Association for the Study of Higher Education, March, Washington, D.C.

Clark, Shirley M., and Corcoran, Mary. 1983. "Professional Socialization and Faculty Career Vitality." Paper presented at the annual meeting of the American Educational Research Association, Division J—Postsecondary Education, April, Montreal.

Coughlin, Ellen K. 21 October 1981. "Scholars See Possible Conflict in Academics' Ties." *Chronicle of Higher Education* 23 (8).

Counelis, James Steve. 1974. "Faculty Professionalism beyond the University Classroom." Unpublished manuscript. Office of Institutional Studies and Management Information, University of San Francisco.

Crosson, Patricia H. 1983. *Public Service in Higher Education: Practices and Priorities.* ASHE-ERIC Higher Education Research Report No. 7. Washington, D.C.: Association for the Study of Higher Education. ED 239 569. 140 pp. MF–$0.97; PC–$12.96.

Dill, David D. 1982. "The Structure of the Academic Profession: Toward a Definition of Ethical Issues." *Journal of Higher Education* 53(3): 255–67.

Dillon, Kristine E. 1979a. "Ethics in Consulting and Outside Professional Activities." Paper presented at the American Association for Higher Education Annual Conference, April, Washington, D.C. ED 183 041. 8 pp. MF–$0.97; PC–$3.54.

———. 1979b. "Outside Professional Activities." *National Forum: Phi Kappa Phi Journal* 69(4): 38–42.

———. 1982. "Economics of the Academic Profession: A Perspective on Total Professional Earnings." In *Dollars and Scholars: An Inquiry into the Impact of Faculty Income upon the Function and Future of the Academy,* edited by Robert H. Linnell. Los Angeles: University of Southern California Press.

Dillon, Kristine E., and Bane, Karen L. 1980. "Consulting and Conflict of Interest: A Compendium of the Policies of Almost One Hundred Major Colleges and Universities." *Educational Record* 61(2): 52–72.

Dillon, Kristine E., and Linnell, Robert H. 1980a. "How and For What Are Professors Paid?" *National Forum: Phi Kappa Phi Journal* 60(2): 21–23.

————. 1980b. "How Well Are Faculty Paid? Implications of the Academic Reward Structure." *Current Issues in Higher Education* 3: 1–11.

Dillon, Kristine E., and Marsh, Herbert W. 1981. "Faculty Earnings Compared with Those of Nonacademic Professionals." *Journal of Higher Education* 52(6): 615–23.

Dunham, R. E.; Wright, P. S.; and Chandler, M. O. 1966. *Teaching Faculty in Universities and Four-Year Colleges*. Washington, D.C.: U.S. Office of Education.

Eddy, Margot Sanders. 1981. "Faculty Response to Retrenchment." *AAHE-ERIC Higher Education Research Currents* 33(10): 7–10. ED 202 446. 5 pp. MF–$0.97; PC–$3.54.

Euster, Gerald L., and Weinbach, Robert W. 1983. "University Rewards for Faculty Community Service." *Journal of Education for Social Work* 19(1): 108–14.

Finkelstein, Martin J. 1978. "Three Decades of Research on American Academics: A Descriptive Portrait and Synthesis of Findings." Ph.D. dissertation, State University of New York–Buffalo.

Freedman, Leonard. 1979. "The Ethics and Economics of Supplemental Teaching." Paper presented at the Fourth Annual Academic Planning Conference, University of Southern California, June, Los Angeles. ED 181 825. 10 pp. MF–$0.97; PC–$3.54.

Fulton, Oliver, and Trow, Martin. 1974. "Research Activity in American Education." *Sociology of Education* 47(1):29–73.

Furniss, W. Todd. 1981. *Reshaping Faculty Careers*. Washington, D.C.: American Council on Education.

Gallessich, June. 1982. *The Profession and Practice of Consultation*. San Francisco: Jossey-Bass.

George, Thomas W. 1976. "Behavior Consultation: A Model for Effective Public Service Involvement." *College Student Journal* 10(2): 131–33.

Glauser, Michael J., and Axley, Stephen R. 1983. "Consulting Activities of University Faculty Members: Scope and Depth of nvolvement." *Group and Organizational Studies* 8(3): 270–86.

Goldberg, Alvin. 1983. "Resolved: That Paid Consulting Is Contrary to the Best Interests of Academia—The Affirmative." *Association for Communication Administration Bulletin* 44: 14–16.

Golomb, Solomon W. 1979. "Faculty Consulting: Should It Be Curtailed?" *National Forum: Phi Kappa Phi Journal* 69(4): 34–37.

Hansen, W. Lee. 1979. "Academic Compensation: Myths and Realities (Revised)." Paper presented at the Fourth Annual

Academic Planning Conference, University of Southern California, June, Los Angeles. ED 181 822. 32 pp. MF–$0.97; PC–$5.34.

————. 1984. "Bottoming Out? Annual Report on the Economic Status of the Profession, 1983–84" (written report of the Committee Z chair). *Academe: Bulletin of the AAUP* 70(2): 3–10.

Hardin, Paul. 1979. "Ethical and Economic Issues in Academe: The Point of View of a University President." Paper presented at the Fourth Annual Academic Planning Conference, University of Southern California, June, Los Angeles. ED 181 821. 8 pp. MF–$0.97; PC–$3.54.

Inman, Virginia. 31 March 1983. "Academia's Experts: Professors Are Taking More Consulting Jobs, with College Approval." *Wall Street Journal.*

Jencks, Christopher, and Riesman, David. 1968. *The Academic Revolution.* New York: Doubleday.

Jolly, David. 1978. "Perspective of California Legislators on Disclosure and Accountability as It Relates to Faculty Salaries and Supplemental Income." Paper presented at the Third Annual Academic Planning Conference, University of Southern California, January, Los Angeles. ED 152 166. 10 pp. MF–$0.97; PC–$3.54.

Kirschling, Wayne R. 1979. "Conceptual Problems and Issues in Academic Labor Productivity." In *Academic Rewards in Higher Education,* edited by Darrell R. Lewis and William E. Becker, Jr. Cambridge, Mass.: Ballinger.

Lacy, Larry W., and others. December 1981. "Activities of Science and Engineering Faculty in Universities and Four-Year Colleges: 1978–79 (Final Report NSF 81-323)." Washington, D.C.: National Science Foundation, Division of Science Resource Studies. ED 221 129. 88 pp. MF–$0.97; PC–$9.36.

Ladd, E. C., Jr. 1978. "The Economic Position of the American Professoriate: A Survey Portrait." Paper presented at the Third Annual Academic Planning Conference, University of Southern California, January, Los Angeles. ED 152 165. 42 pp. MF–$0.97; PC–$5.34.

Ladd, E. C., and Lipset, S. M. 1975a. *The Divided Academy: Professors and Politics.* New York: McGraw-Hill.

————. 1975b. *Technical Report: 1975 Survey of the American Professoriate.* Storrs, Conn.: University of Connecticut, Social Science Data Center.

Lajoie, M. Stephen, and Weinberg, Myron S. 1978. "Industrial Views of Faculty Research Services." Paper presented at the Third Annual Academic Planning Conference, University of

Southern California, January, Los Angeles. ED 152 203. 27 pp. MF–$0.97; PC–$5.34.

Langway, Lynn, and others. 1978. "Too Much Moonlighting?" *Newsweek* 92(1): 84.

Lanning, Alan W. 1977. "Some Correlates of Paid Faculty Consultants at Major Universities: An Analysis of Their Cosmopolitan Local Orientation." Ph.D. dissertation, University of Michigan.

Lanning, Alan, and Blackburn, Robert T. 1979. "Faculty Consulting and the Consultant." *Resources in Education* 14: 107. ED 160 024. 47 pp. MF–$0.97; PC–$5.34.

Lewis, Darrell R., and Becker, William E., Jr., eds. 1979. *Academic Rewards in Higher Education*. Cambridge, Mass.: Ballinger.

Lewis, Darrell R., and Kellogg, Theodore E. 1979. "Planning and Evaluation Criteria for Allocating Departmental and Collegiate Resources in a University Setting." In *Academic Rewards in Higher Education,* edited by Darrell R. Lewis and William E. Becker, Jr. Cambridge, Mass.: Ballinger.

Light, Donald, Jr. 1974. "Introduction: The Structure of the Academic Professions." *Sociology of Education* 47(1): 2–28.

Linnell, Robert H., ed. 1982. *Dollars and Scholars: An Inquiry into the Impact of Faculty Income upon the Function and Future of the Academy*. Los Angeles: University of Southern California Press.

Linnell, Robert H., and Marsh, Herbert W. 1977. "Ethical and Economic Issues: An Interview Survey at Ten Universities." Paper presented at the Second Annual Academic Planning Conference, University of Southern California, January, Los Angeles. ED 136 729. 26 pp. MF–$0.97; PC–$5.34.

Lipset, Seymour Martin. 1982. "The Academic Mind at the Top: The Political Behavior and Values of Faculty Elites." *Public Opinion Quarterly* 46: 143–68.

Longenecker, Herbert E. 1956. *University Faculty Compensation Policies and Practices in the United States*. Urbana, Ill.: University of Illinois Press for the Association of American Universities.

Lumsden, Keith, and Ritchie, C. 1975. "The Open University: A Survey and Economic Analysis." *Instructional Science* 4: 237–92.

McGough, Bobby. 1969. "How Much Time Should Faculty Spend on 'Outside' Consulting? Policies Vary with Size of Institution." *College and University Business* 46(5): 30–34.

Marsh, Herbert W., and Dillon, Kristine E. 1980. "Academic Productivity and Faculty Supplemental Income." *Journal of Higher Education* 51(5): 546–55.

Martin, Warren Bryan, ed. 1977. *Redefining Service, Research, and Teaching*. New Directions for Higher Education No. 18. San Francisco: Jossey-Bass.

Marver, James D., and Patton, Carl Vernon. 1976. "The Correlates of Consultation: American Academics in 'The Real World.' " *Higher Education* 5(3): 319–35.

National Education Association. 1953. *Salary Schedule Provisions or Salaries Paid in Degree-Granting Institutions*. Washington, D.C.: Author.

———. 1956 through 1964. *Salaries Paid and Salary Practices in Universities, Colleges, and Junior Colleges*. Washington, D.C.: Author.

———. 1966 through 1972. *Salaries in Higher Education or Salaries Paid and Salary-Related Practices in Higher Education*. Washington, D.C.: Author.

National Research Council. 1982. *Science, Engineering, and Humanities Doctorates in the United States: 1981 Profile*. Washington, D.C.: National Academy Press. ED 230 389. 82 pp. MF–$0.97; PC not available EDRS.

National Science Foundation. 1977. *Characteristics of Doctoral Scientists and Engineers in the United States, 1975*. Washington, D.C.: U.S. Government Printing Office. ED 141 181. 224 pp. MF–$0.97; PC not available EDRS.

New York Times. 8 February 1983. "Coast Teachers Warned on Ties to Corporations."

Nocks, Barry C. 1982. "Academicians as Consultants: Traveling between Two Cultures." Unpublished manuscript, South Carolina. ED 225 444. 12 pp. MF–$0.97; PC–$3.54.

Parsons, Talcott, and Platt, Gerald M. 1968. *The American Academic Profession: A Pilot Study*. Cambridge, Mass.: Harvard University Press.

Patton, Carl V. 1980. "Consulting by Faculty Members." *Academe: Bulletin of the AAUP* 66(4): 181–85.

Patton, Carl V., and Marver, James D. 1979. "Paid Consulting by American Academics." *Educational Record* 60(2): 175–84.

Perkins, James A. 1973. "Organization and Functions of the University." In *The University as an Organization,* edited by James A. Perkins. New York: McGraw-Hill.

Pilon, Daniel H., and Bergquist, William H. 1979. *Consultation in Higher Education: A Handbook for Practitioners and Clients,* edited by Gary H. Quehl and Jean Brodsky. Washington, D.C.:

Council for the Advancement of Small Colleges. ED 183 042. 161 pp. MF–$0.97; PC not available EDRS.

Redding, W. Charles. 1983. "Resolved: That Paid Consulting Is Contrary to the Best Interests of Academia—The Negative." *Association for Communication Administration Bulletin* 44: 17–20.

Roizen, Judith; Fulton, Oliver; and Trow, Martin. 1978. *Technical Report: 1975 Carnegie Council National Survey of Higher Education*. Berkeley: University of California, Center for Studies in Higher Education.

Schurr, George H. 1979. "Toward a Code of Ethics for Academics." Unpublished manuscript. University of Delaware, Center for the Study of Values. ED 181 795. 29 pp. MF–$0.97; PC–$5.34.

Schwartz, Lois. 1980. "Ethical Issues in Consulting." *NSPI Journal* 19(9): 40–43.

Scientific Manpower Commission. 1964, 1971, 1977. *Salaries of Scientists, Engineers, and Technicians*. Washington, D.C. American Association for the Advancement of Science.

Seiler, William J., and Dunning, David. 1983. "Communication Consulting from Academe to the 'Real World.' " Paper presented at the Annual Meeting of the Central States Speech Association, April, Lincoln, Nebraska. ED 234 442. 18 pp. MF–$0.97; PC–$3.54.

Shulman, Carol Herrnstadt. 1980. "Faculty Ethics: New Dilemmas, New Choices." *AAHE-ERIC Higher Education Research Currents* 32(10): 7–10. ED 187 290. 5 pp. MF–$0.97; PC–$3.54.

Simon, Herbert A. 1976. *Administrative Behavior*. 3d ed. New York: The Free Press.

Stigler, George J. 1950. *Employment and Compensation in Education*. New York: National Bureau of Economic Research.

Teague, Gerald V. 1982. "Faculty Consulting: Do Universities Have 'Control'?" *Research in Higher Education* 17(2): 179–86.

Thompson, Mark S. 1980. *Benefit-Cost Analysis for Program Evaluation*. Beverly Hills, Cal.: Sage Publications.

Tickton, Sidney G. 1961. *Teaching Salaries Then and Now—A Second Look*. New York: Fund for the Advancement of Education (Ford Foundation).

Trivett, David A. 1978. "Compensation in Higher Education." *AAHE-ERIC Research Currents*. Washington, D.C.: American Association for Higher Education. ED 150 914. 5 pp. MF–$0.97; PC–$3.54.

Trow, Martin. 1972. *Technical Report: National Survey of Higher Education*. Berkeley, Cal.: Carnegie Commission on Higher

Education. ED 066 114. 132 pp. MF–$0.97; PC–$12.96.

Tuckman, Howard P. 1984. "Book review of *Dollars and Scholars: An Inquiry into the Impact of Faculty Income upon the Function and Future of the Academy,* edited by Robert H. Linnell." *Journal of Higher Education* 55(3): 430–32.

University of Minnesota. July 1980. "A Mission and Policy Statement for the University of Minnesota." Minneapolis: Author.

Voegel, George. 1977. "Ethical and Economic Issues: Intellectual Property, Who Owns It?" Paper presented at the Second Annual Academic Planning Conference, University of Southern California, January, Los Angeles. ED 138 169. 17 pp. MF–$0.97; PC–$3.54.

Weston, Michael C. 1980–81. " 'Outside' Activities of Faculty Members." *Journal of College and University Law* 7(1–2): 68–77.

Wildavsky, Aaron. 1978. "Viewpoint 2: The Debate over Faculty Consulting." *Change* 10(6): 13–14.

Wilson, Logan. 1942. *The Academic Man.* New York: Oxford University Press.

———. 1972. "The Professor and His Roles" (lecture given 15 September 1965 at the University of Michigan, Ann Arbor). In *Shaping American Higher Education,* by Logan Wilson. Washington, D.C.: American Council on Education.

———. 1979. *American Academics: Then and Now.* New York: Oxford University Press.

Wolfle, Dael. 1972. *The Home of Science: The Role of the University.* New York: McGraw-Hill.

Woodrow, Raymond J. 1978. "Inventions and Information in Faculty Consulting Relationships." Paper presented at the Third Annual Academic Planning Conference, University of Southern California, January, Los Angeles. ED 152 162. 8 pp. MF–$0.97; PC–$3.54.

INDEX

A

AAUP (see American Association of University Professors)
"Academic man" as "economic man," 42–43
Academic freedom: abuse of, 13
Academic-year consulting, 18–20, 36
Accountability, 50
ACE (see American Council on Education)
American Association of University Professors (AAUP), 25–26, 37, 48, 49, 50
American Council on Education (ACE), 15, 48, 49, 50
"Annual Report on the Economic Status of the Profession," 25, 28, 32

B

Benefits
       cost tradeoffs, 7–9
       to society, 11–12
       to the individual, 9–10
       to the institution, 10–11
Bioengineering, 13
Business faculty, 22

C

Carnegie Commission, 15
Chronicle of Higher Education, 26
Community colleges: policy, 52–53
Compensation, 26, 37
Computer electronics, 13
Conflict of interest, 13, 48
Consulting
       as form of service, 4
       cost effectiveness, 7–13
       definition, 3–5
       description, 46–48
       extent of, 16–23
       historical context, 2
       implications for policy, 55–56
       literature on, 1
       motivation, 42
       national surveys, 15–16, 56–57
       policies on, 45–53
       potential benefits, 9–12
Consumer Price Index (CPI): and faculty salaries, 26, 28
Contracts and grants: benefit to institutions, 11
Copyrights, 13

Guidelines (see Institutional policy)

H
Harvard University, 13
Higher Education General Information Survey (HEGIS), 26
Historical context, 2
Humanities faculty, 22, 35, 36, 37

I
Incidence of consulting, 17–20
Income (see Supplemental income)
Institutional mission
      and supplemental income, 1–2
      teaching/research/service tradition, 3
Institutional policy
      four-year colleges/community colleges, 52–53
      limitations/regulations, 48–51
      major colleges/universities, 46–52
      need for revision, 55–56
      permission required/procedures, 51–52
      surveys, 45
Institutional resources: use of, 13
Intellectual property rights, 13

J
Johns Hopkins University, 2
Junior college faculty, 19

K
Knowledge transfer, 12

L
Land grant universities: and idea of service, 2
Law faculty, 22
Limitations, 46–51
Lincoln (Abraham), 2
Local business: consultants to, 22
Local government: consultants to, 22

M
"Market retention" of faculty, 10
Maryland, 53
Maryse Eymonerie Associates, 26
Medical faculty, 17, 22
Minter (John) Associates, 26

"Moonlighting": definition, 4–5
"The more, the more" concept, 23
Morrill Land Grant Act of 1862, 2

N

National Center for Education Statistics (NCES), 25, 26, 57
National Endowment for the Humanities (NEH), 27
National Institutes of Health (NIH), 27
National Research Council (NRC), 16, 18, 19, 27, 57
National Science Foundation (NSF), 16, 18, 27, 57
National surveys, 15–16
NCES (see National Center for Education Statistics)
NEH (see National Endowment for the Humanities)
NIH (see National Institutes of Health)
NRC (see National Research Council)
NSF (see National Science Foundation)

O

"Opportunity costs," 7–8
Overload income, 25

P

Paid versus unpaid consulting, 17–20
Patents, 13, 35
Permission required/procedures, 51–52
Philosophy faculty, 17
Policy (see Institutional policy)
Policy review/revision, 46
Policy statement (AAUP-ACE), 48, 49
Prior approval by institutions, 51–52
Productivity, 17, 22–23, 55–56
Professional versus nonprofessional fields, 19, 21
Psychology faculty, 17
Public service, 1, 2, 48
Publishing activity, 22–23, 35

R

Regulations, 46–51
Reporting requirement, 52
Research needs, 56–58
Research universities
    and idea of service, 2
    as consultant base, 21
Researchers, active: consulting role, 17, 22
Responsibility/accountability, 22–23
Royalties, 34, 35

ASHE-ERIC HIGHER EDUCATION REPORTS

Starting in 1983, the Association for the Study of Higher Education assumed cosponsorship of the Higher Education Reports with the ERIC Clearinghouse on Higher Education. For the previous 11 years, ERIC and the American Association for Higher Education prepared and published the reports.

Each report is the definitive analysis of a tough higher education problem, based on a thorough research of pertinent literature and institutional experiences. Report topics, identified by a national survey, are written by noted practitioners and scholars with prepublication manuscript reviews by experts.

Eight monographs (10 monographs before 1985) in the ASHE-ERIC Higher Education Report series are published each year, available individually or by subscription. Subscription to eight issues is $55 regular; $40 for members of AERA, AAHE and AIR: $35 for members of ASHE. (Add $7.50 outside the United States.)

Prices for single copies, including 4th class postage and handling, are $7.50 regular and $6.00 for members of AERA, AAHE, AIR, and ASHE ($6.50 regular and $5.00 for members for reports published before 1983). If faster 1st class postage is desired for U.S. and Canadian orders, add $.75 for each publication ordered: overseas, add $4.50. For VISA and MasterCard payments, include card number, expiration date, and signature. Orders under $25 must be prepaid. Bulk discounts are available on orders of 15 or more reports (not applicable to subscriptions). Order from the Publications Department, Association for the Study of Higher Education, One Dupont Circle, Suite 630, Washington, D.C. 20036, (202 296-2597. Write for a publication list of all the Higher Education Reports available.

1985 Higher Education Reports

1. Flexibility in Academic Staffing: Effective Policies and Practices
   Kenneth P. Mortimer, Marque Bagshaw, and Andrew T. Masland

2. Associations in Action: The Washington, D.C., Higher Education Community
   Harland G. Bloland

3. And on the Seventh Day: Faculty Consulting and Supplemental Income
   Carol M. Boyer and Darrell R. Lewis

1984 Higher Education Reports

1. Adult Learning: State Policies and Institutional Practices
   K. Patricia Cross and Anne-Marie McCartan

2. Student Stress: Effects and Solutions
   Neal A. Whitmar, David C. Spendlove, and Claire H. Clark

3. Part-time Faculty: Higher Education at a Crossroads
   Judith M. Gappa

4. Sex Discrimination Law in Higher Education: The Lessons of the Past Decade
   J. Ralph Lindgren, Patti T. Ota, Perry A. Zirkel, and Nan Van Gieson